THE JESUS OF MARK'S GOSPEL

Westminster Press Books by

Dorothy M. and Gerald H. Slusser
THE JESUS OF MARK'S GOSPEL

Gerald H. Slusser
THE LOCAL CHURCH IN TRANSITION:
THEOLOGY, EDUCATION, AND MINISTRY

Dorothy M. Slusser
AT THE FOOT OF THE MOUNTAIN:
STORIES FROM THE BOOK OF EXODUS
BIBLE STORIES RETOLD FOR ADULTS

The Jesus
of
Mark's Gospel

43

by

Dorothy M. Slusser

and

Gerald H. Slusser

BS
2585.3
.S58

The Westminster Press
Philadelphia

LIBRARY OF CONGRESS CATALOG CARD NO. 68–10227

PUBLISHED BY THE WESTMINSTER PRESS®
PHILADELPHIA, PENNSYLVANIA

PRINTED IN THE UNITED STATES OF AMERICA

CONTENTS

INTRODUCTION

IF MARK'S GOSPEL were all that remained as a witness to the Christ event, we would largely be left to wonder about the nature of the Kingdom of God about which he speaks. His Gospel contains almost no teaching material, or even what the word was that Jesus brought in his teaching and preaching which could have produced the profound effect which it did. If the reader did not have access to the remainder of the New Testament, he would have no clear idea of what the good news consisted, other than a few passing references to the moral law such as the Ten Commandments and the proper attitude toward divorce, etc. Mark does not talk about *what* the good news is, but *who* it is that brings it and for *whom* it is intended. For example, except for the episode in which the first and second greatest commandments are given, the word "love" appears at no other point in the Gospel, and even here Mark does not speak of God's love for man, but rather of the necessity of man's love for God and fellowman. The Gospel is concerned to witness that Jesus was the bearer of God's reconciliation, but simply taking the surface of Mark's book, one would have to assume that Mark's readers already knew the good news of that reconciliation. It would appear that Mark did not feel it necessary to include such material directly. He wrote to an audience that apparently was capable of understanding the nature of

God's covenant with man through a thorough understanding of the Old Testament itself and any details of Jesus' teaching and preaching on these matters were simply not germane to the purpose that he had in mind.

There are really two very different and quite contradictory Old Testament traditions concerning Israel's call by God to covenant. There is the tradition that follows the Genesis pattern, with the calling of and covenant with Abraham, which can be found most clearly in such books as Isaiah, Jeremiah, some of the Minor Prophets, and Ruth and Jonah. Then there is the tradition that follows the Deuteronomic pattern, stemming from the reform of Josiah with emphasis on the Law, which is found most clearly represented in such books as Deuteronomy, Nehemiah, Ezra, etc. It is the difference between these two traditions which is seen in operation in the Gospel of Mark, viz., on the one hand, the understanding that was embraced by the professional leaders of Judaism and shared by the populace, and on the other hand, that which Jesus as the Son of God brought and preached to his disciples and which was a threat to the orthodox Judaism of that day. Jesus' teaching in Mark consists almost entirely of how the word from God will be received and what manner of servant is required by God for fulfilling the *true* covenant. Most of the teaching concerns the ultimate demise of Judaism, and Jesus' teaching to the disciples is completely taken up with this and their roles as substitutes for it.

Much of the meaning of the Gospel of Mark was lost very early because it depends upon a complex set of symbols and references, taken in large measure from the Old Testament. It is the thesis of this book that the *full* meaning of Mark's Gospel has scarcely been heard since he wrote it. This book has been a long time in gestation and labor because it was so difficult to decide how to make

Mark's meaning manifest in a book of reasonable length. It was decided that no attempts should be made to write a technical work for two reasons: First, most of the data of such a work are already available in the technical literature of the New Testament field; but secondly, and more important, we think that new insight into Scripture, such as we believe this book to be, should be made readily available to the clergy and laity of the church and not only to scholars. The attempts to fulfill this latter aim meant that strenuous effort had to be made to avoid many of the small technical issues that plague most serious commentaries. It meant also that, at times, background data had to be provided which would not be needed by the New Testament scholar. It was also resolved, in order to give maximum attention to Mark's structure and meaning, to avoid exposition or application of Scripture. This latter entailed rather sparse treatment of what teaching material is included in the book, where the meaning does not depend upon symbolic reference.

It does not seem necessary to make a case for many assumptions that have been made about various circumstances of the writing of the Gospel when these assumptions do not materially affect the conclusions reached. For example, the author of the Gospel is assumed to be John Mark, who accompanied Paul and later, presumably, served as a secretary to Peter, but no conclusions are based on this assumption. When the assumptions appear to affect conclusions, the relevant scholarly apparatus has been included.

As indicated, we believe this book to be a new approach to the Gospel of Mark. Many have dismissed Mark's Gospel as a mere patchwork of reminiscences put together by a semiliterate and somewhat careless editor (although, there have been some recent works that depart from this earlier position, e.g., Austin Farrer, R. H. Lightfoot, John

Bowman, etc.). We believe the case to be quite the contrary. Mark's work, we shall attempt to show, was a carefully engineered piece of literary art done by a man of great skill with an extraordinary knowledge of the Old Testament and its subtleties. Each part is fashioned with skill and woven into a carefully patterned whole. Mark had an overall plan like the plot of a drama, but, we believe, his intention was not that of a dramatist, a biographer, or a historian. His purpose was to set forth the meaning of the life of Jesus as he understood it. He was presenting his understanding of Jesus as the Christ.

Immediately, the question of the relation of Mark's account to the actual events of Jesus' life is raised, requiring another crucial decision about this book. Recently, the New Testament scholars of the "new quest" (for the historical Jesus) school have been emphasizing the possibility (and usually they say the necessity) of recovering a faithful picture of Jesus as *the* man of faith as a basis for our faith. The possibility of success in this venture is being hotly debated. We do not believe, however, that it is necessary to enter this argument in order to accomplish the purposes of our commentary on Mark. It is not known now, and may never be, just how accurately, in the newspaper reporter sense, Mark re-presented the details of Jesus' life or faith. We believe that Mark used historical events as symbols whose meaning is not dependent upon the fact that they happened. We believe also that at times he rearranged names, places, and situations to give these symbolic significance, but which parts are accidents of history and which parts are poetic imagery is rarely discoverable. Thus, our commentary is intended to unveil the meaning of Mark's Gospel by unraveling his complex pattern and symbolism and showing its intent. There will be no attempt to penetrate behind what Mark has given to get at "what really happened," although at many points the reader may choose to draw conclusions about the historical reality of Mark's narrative. Did all these events really happen as they are described? Did Mark invent some or many of them? Such questions are finally not only probably unanswerable, but answers are not necessary for Christian faith. Interesting historical questions, yes, but only that.

Mark's Gospel portrays the mounting tension between Jesus and the professional leadership of Israel from his first teaching to his ultimate condemnation. While it is the story of the life and death of Jesus, it is no less the story of the death of the orthodox Judaism of that day, in Mark's view. Coming where it does in the Gospel, the parable of the vineyard and the tenants captures the *raison d'être* for Mark's Gospel. In unmistakably clear symbolism, Mark's Jesus revealed God's judgment of the leaders of Israel, who recognized themselves as the wicked tenants. The parable and its revelation became the final straw with the priests, and from henceforth the destruction of Jesus was foregone, waiting only a practical resolution. That the Christian community had Jesus Christ at its head, instead of the Judaistic priesthood, as the prophecy in the parable claimed, was a fact of historical knowledge for Mark.

The Gospel illustrates Jesus' largely unsuccessful attempt to pass along to a small group of followers his understanding of the call to fulfill the covenant with God. Jesus was even less successful in convincing those followers of the kind of servant each must become to serve God in his covenant. Much of Jesus' ministry in Mark occurs on the periphery of the Jewish community and in Gentile country. In the end the disciples fall away, and after Jesus' death they do not appear in this Gospel. Word from Jesus is passed along to them through the women who visited the tomb. The women are told by the young man there that Jesus had already gone before them into Galilee of the Gentiles where he would meet them.

Our first thanks go to Professor Edward Hobbs, the Church Divinity School of the Pacific, whose own interest in the Gospel of Mark was responsible for ours. Our personal thanks go to Mrs. Walter Brueggemann for her volunteer services as a valuable proofreader.

DOROTHY M. SLUSSER
GERALD H. SLUSSER

St. Louis, Missouri

Chapter 1

THE BEGINNING OF THE GOSPEL

Mark 1:1–15

THE TASK AT HAND is to try to make explicit that which Mark has left implicit, and still understand his Gospel with his own understanding, completely apart from the understanding of subsequent writers and interpreters. One of the first things to be discovered in this attempt is Mark's rare use of actual quotations of Old Testament Scripture. Where it often appears that Mark has given us a quotation, it is many times revealed that he has not *exactly* quoted any one passage but, by an ingenious use of words, has made allusion to several different passages. By so doing, he will have linked together in one statement the Law, the Prophets, and the apocalypses. You could almost say that he "makes up" his quotations, and by connecting the phrases of several passages, he has also connected the meanings inherent in these diverse but related passages. Now, we do this also. When we are discussing Biblical "doctrine," we gather together various passages relating to it to set forth a Biblical theology. In this sense, Mark can be called a theologian of the Old Testament, arranging his material in the light of the life of Jesus Christ.

The Prophecy

At the outset, the reader finds himself thrust successively into the books of Exodus, Malachi, and Isaiah. The quotation from the prophecy of Isaiah is prefaced by one from Exodus—or nearly a quotation from Exodus. The order of material, law followed by prophecy, was one traditional with the scribes in the synagogue, where the Prophets were not usually read except as commentary on the Law. But Mark's adherence to tradition, if that is the correct interpretation, is, as we will come to expect of him, one with a difference. The words which at first glance appear to be a quotation of Ex. 23:20 are these:

> Behold, I send my messenger before thy face,
> who shall prepare thy way.
>
> (Mark 1:2.)

The Exodus passage reads:

> Behold, I send an angel before you, to guard you on the way and to bring you to the place which I have prepared.
>
> (Ex. 23:20.)

Angels are, of course, God's messengers, but even the substitution of "messenger" for "angel" in this passage will not allow the reader to believe that this is an exact quotation. On the other hand, a look at the final book in the Old Testament canon, which has been traditionally regarded as the source of Mark's quotation, forces the admission that Mark has not *exactly* quoted from Malachi (which name also means "messenger"). The words from Mal. 3:1 are these:

> Behold, I send my messenger to prepare the way before me.

What Mark appears to have done is to combine the Exodus passage with that from Malachi, and thereby subtly called to his reader's attention vastly more than that which a simple use of the verse from Malachi would have done. If it is Mark's intention that the reader should think of both "ends" of Israelite history and understanding, then not only should one look for something new to happen to fulfill the prophecy in Malachi but one should expect the something new to be connected with something old—the historical and religious pivot of Israel's history: the exodus from Egypt. Only after guiding one's thought through both the history and expectation of Israel in one sentence, does Mark actually quote, as he has promised, from Isaiah:

> The voice of one crying in the wilderness:
> Prepare the way of the LORD,
> make his paths straight.
>
> (Isa. 40:3; Mark 1:3.)

Exodus, or deliverance by God, is the one continuing emphasis in the Old Testament. God delivered Adam, his child Everyman, from the waters and the darkness at the creation (Gen., chs. 1 to 3). Again, under the leadership of Moses, Israel, God's son, had been delivered through the waters into the wilderness from captivity in Egypt (Ex. 14:10 ff.). Once more God delivered Israel out of the wilderness into the Promised Land through the waters of the Jordan under the leadership of Joshua (Josh. 3:7 ff.).

Having settled in the land, Israel had turned for meaning in her life to some source other than God, and her disloyalty had culminated in captivity and exile into Babylon. God's voice came to her through the prophets, calling Israel back to him. Isaiah told Israel that her deliverance from Babylon would be effected by God, who would stretch a smooth highway across the impassable desert. The desert would rejoice and bloom, the valleys would be lifted up and the mountains lowered. The uneven ground he would level and the rough country he would transform into a plain (Isa. 40:4).

Thus, with a few words, Mark has set the stage for his Gospel in terms recalling God's repeated deliverance of Israel. As God had acted to effect Israel's deliverance before, he could be expected to do so again. (For the clarification of our readers, where we refer to the nation as Israel, we shall do so in the feminine gender, even though we speak of "her" as God's "son." The Book of Hosea speaks of Israel, the nation, as God's bride in much the same manner in which the New Testament speaks of the Christian church. Where, however, we apply the term "Israel" to Jesus, we will, of course, use the masculine gender.)

Having dropped us into the Old Testament, and given us an expectation concerning the role of Jesus Christ, Mark begins his account of the messenger. The concluding verses of Malachi, and hence of the Old Testament itself, establish both the identity and the work of the messenger:

> Behold, I will send you Elijah the prophet before the great and terrible day of the LORD comes.
>
> (Mal. 4:5.)

Any reference to the messenger includes implicitly a reference to the event that he heralds—an exodus of deliverance which the Jews had come to associate with the idea of the "day of the LORD." The prophecy of Malachi identifies the messenger who is to prepare the way for the day of the Lord as Elijah, and it was a common belief that Israel's deliverer, the Messiah, was to have Elijah as his forerunner.

The age immediately prior to the advent of Jesus Christ was an age without prophecy, but not because there were no voices raised in clamor of judgment and expectation. The great wealth of apocryphal literature amply testifies to that fact. That there was a resistance to prophecy is well established, whether one refers to the classic works of R. H. Charles[1] or turns to more recent works.[2] What amounted almost to deliberate suppression of prophecy by the priesthood altered the shout from the lips of the prophets, "Thus saith the Lord," to the tame, quiet, scholarly voice of the scribes who read in the synagogues, "Thus reads the Law."

The Prophetic Herald

The age had come officially, therefore, to accept the end of prophecy (cf. Zech. 13:2 f.). As we live in an age that no longer expects the "miraculous," so men then lived in a postprophetic age. Haggai, Zechariah, and Malachi were considered to be the last writers to receive divine inspiration. If anyone had a message for Israel which he deemed prophetic in nature, he generally wrote it under a pseudonym chosen from the earlier prophets and formulated the work in a style and historical setting compatible with his choice, e.g., Deutero-Isaiah.

Nothing would be more natural to Israel as she looked forward to a new day of deliverance predicted by the last of the prophets than to cast Elijah into the role of forerunner—he who had not died but had been taken up to heaven alive. There was in Judaistic tradition the acceptance that Elijah would be the forerunner, "and it is presupposed in the Gospels as a common Jewish belief."[3]

There were other forerunners mentioned also, and commonly Elijah's appearance was to include the presence of Moses. Moses and Elijah are the two Old Testament prophets par excellence. God had promised that he would always send a prophet like Moses when the need arose (Deut. 18:15). And, indeed, Moses' appearance is added to that of Elijah in Mark's story of the transfiguration.

It is Elijah whom Mark has led his reader to expect, but it is John the Baptist who strides onto the stage, preaching a baptism of repentance for the forgiveness of sins. Although it is not Elijah who actually appears, it is he who appears symbolically in the person of John. Every facet of John's life, as told by Mark, including his ultimate defeat by a modern Jezebel (Herodias) illustrates the parallel. John, like Elijah, came out of the wilderness preaching repentance to a sinful people. During the time of Elijah, King Ahab of Israel, under the influence of his wife, Jezebel, a worshiper of Baal, had forsaken the worship of God. Under Ahab, Israel had become materialistic, and she was called by Elijah to repent and turn back to God. So John came to Israel, telling her she must again repent and turn to God.

Mark uses even John's attire to aid in his identification as Elijah, relying on the reader to recall a story in the Old Testament about King Ahaziah. During an illness the king sent out messengers to seek prophecy from Baalzebub concerning his health. They returned to him with a message from God which informed the king that he would die. The king asked the messengers what manner of man had given them this unhappy word, and their answer was, "He wore a garment of haircloth, with a girdle of leather about his loins" (II Kings 1:8). Ahaziah recognized immediately of whom they spoke. "It is Elijah the Tishbite," he said. When Mark describes John, saying that he was "clothed with camel's hair, and had a leather girdle around his waist" (Mark 1:6), he surely expects his reader to echo Ahaziah, "It is Elijah the Tishbite." Later in the Gospel, Mark's Jesus confirmed John's identity as Elijah (ch. 9:13).

Mark's use of the Old Testament to illustrate his understanding of the meaning of the Christ event is not unique in the New Testament. Matthew and Luke, not to mention Paul, were similarly oriented. Luke leans more heavily on Genesis than on the exodus,[4] but the meaning of the entire New Testament is firmly anchored by its writers in an understanding of the Old Testament as a whole.

Mark's physical description of John is followed by a sample of his preaching. Concerning the baptism of repentance which he brought, he preached a greater baptism to follow. John's audience was a people whose political and economic independence had been destroyed, and whose lives were bound up in a law that had arisen out of a cultural situation no longer extant. Even though much of that law was therefore obsolete, it was nevertheless artificially preserved and expounded. The Jews prided themselves on being a righteous and godly people, and they regarded their very existence as a people as the fulfillment of a godly purpose and promise. Even though John had a popular following, there were many of his contemporaries who would regard his preaching of a baptism of repentance as an offense. He could scarcely be accepted as a popular leader by a people who prided themselves on keeping the law. Preaching the necessity of repentance would have been affront enough, but to add to this the necessity of baptism would certainly be most unappealing to a great number of people. The function of baptism was regarded by tradition as one of cleansing. Vessels and sacrifices used in Temple worship were first prepared by washing; proselytes from among the Gentiles, and therefore regarded as unclean, were baptized before being accepted into the community. The symbol of cleansing by water stood not only for the washing away of the past, the old life, but also as a preparation for the future, a new life.

Israel's anticipation of the Messiah included the belief that he would come in power and glory and, with a sweep of divine leadership, elevate Israel to her rightful pinnacle above the nations. She had jealously preserved the Temple and kept the fulfilling of the law before her as the instrument for the perfection of her righteousness. With such an understanding of herself and her divine destiny, to be told that she needed to repent of her old self to make way for a new self, to have her old self cleansed away in baptism and be forgiven for her sins, would clearly be unpopular. John further preached that his cleansing would be insufficient to restore her broken relationship to God. Baptism by water must be followed by a baptism of the spirit. John's baptism was simply a preparation for a baptism to come. One greater than he would follow, through whom Israel would receive the baptism of the Holy Spirit.

Jesus from Nazareth

The establishment of John as messenger, the new Elijah, and the introduction of his preaching message is followed, in one of Mark's typically abrupt transitions, by the appearance of Jesus. Although John had declared himself to be less than Jesus, Jesus submitted himself to the hands of John for baptism. As Mark's anticipated deliverer, even Jesus' name is surprisingly appropriate. It is the same as that of the leader chosen to deliver Israel into the Promised Land after the death of Moses. "Take Joshua the son of Nun, a man in whom is the spirit, and lay your hand upon him." (Num. 27:18.) Accordingly, "Joshua," or "Jesus" (the Hebrew and the Greek), was chosen to complete the work begun by Moses.

A "Joshua" appears again in The Book of Zechariah. Zechariah 3:1 states, "Then he showed me Joshua the high priest standing before the angel of the LORD," and here in Mark, Jesus stood before the "messenger." Verse 7 further states that the Lord declared if Joshua would walk in God's ways, he would have the "right of access" to God and the court of heaven. The conquering hero of the prophecy of Zechariah, which concerns the return of the Israelite exiles from Babylon, was Zerubbabel, who, together with Joshua, son of Jehozadak, worked on the rebuilding of the Temple at Jerusalem. But in fact, Mark knew that the name of Zerubbabel had died with the historical events immediately following the return of the exiles to Jerusalem, so when he remembered these words:

Hear now, O Joshua the high priest, you and your friends
who sit before you, for they are men of good omen:
behold, I will bring my servant the Branch. For behold,
upon the stone which I have set before Joshua, upon a
single stone with seven facets, I will engrave its inscrip-
tion, says the LORD of hosts, and I will remove the guilt
of this land in a single day

(Zech. 3:8 f.)

he might very well ask how these words might enlighten
his understanding of the life and teaching of Jesus, and
it would be natural to make use of any such Old Testament passages in this same manner.

Mark apparently considered Jesus' origin of equal symbolic significance with his name. Mark states that Jesus
came from Nazareth of Galilee, the place Matthew identifies as the chosen home of Joseph and Mary, Jesus'
parents, upon their return from the flight into Egypt.
Although there is disagreement among contemporary
scholars as to whether Jesus might be called a "Nazarene"
on the basis of his home "Nazareth,"[5] Mark specifically
calls his reader's attention to Jesus' origin. There is no
really satisfactory way to settle the philological argument
with any finality concerning the correctness of deriving
"Nazarene" from "Nazareth," but the possibility is an
open one, and as a matter of fact, Matthew does so
(Matt. 2:23).

One Hebrew root of the word "nazarene" means "shoot"
or "branch," and such a reference would lead Mark's
reader to the passage in Isaiah, traditionally interpreted as
messianic:

There shall come forth a shoot from the stump of Jesse,
and a branch shall grow out of his roots.
And the Spirit of the LORD shall rest upon him.

(Isa. 11:1 f.)

The term "branch" was mentioned above in conjunction with "Joshua" in the passage from Zechariah which states that the Lord said, "I will bring my servant the Branch." Assuming that Mark intended to refer the reader to the passage in Isaiah by stating that Jesus was from Nazareth, it must be treated as relevant to Mark's understanding of the character of Jesus.

The section of Isaiah's prophecy paints a picture of the work Israel could expect to see proceeding from the "shoot." Through him the earth was to be filled with the knowledge of the Lord like the waters covering the sea; he would stand as a banner to the people, and the nations would seek him; he would gather the nations together with the outcasts of Israel, gathering the dispersed from the four corners of the earth. Isaiah was particularly speaking of the "remnant" whom God was going to deliver, and he says that Israel's place in the sun would be assured by the work of the "shoot" or "branch" as he carried out the will of God, and the nations would, by his advent, be brought to submission before God (Isa. 11:9 ff.).

Since it was a common Hebrew belief that a man's name denoted his character and personality, it would not be unnatural for Mark to attach Jesus' name to a word he intended to use as a symbol. Mark treats the Old Testament not merely as a historical document but as a light that could shed understanding on the life and mission of Jesus.

The Baptism

By the time Mark wrote, baptism was an established practice in the Christian community, and in the book of The Acts it is associated with the gift of the Holy Spirit. When Jesus offered himself for baptism at John's hand, Mark states that he came up out of the water and God's Spirit came to rest on him, exactly as prophesied in the passage in Isaiah concerning the "branch." Mark further states that a Voice came from the opened heavens, saying, "Thou art my beloved Son; with thee I am well pleased" (ch. 1:11). The words reflect the meaning but are not a specific quotation of several Old Testament passages, e.g., Ps. 2:7; Isa. 42:1; Jer. 31:20; and perhaps even Gen. 22:2.

Their nearest equivalent is found in Isa. 42:1: "Behold my servant, whom I uphold, my chosen, in whom my soul delights; I have put my Spirit upon him." The Old Testament manuscript at Mark's hand probably was the Septuagint, the original Hebrew translated into Greek. It reads at this point: "Israel, my elect, Jacob, my Son, whom I uphold. . . ." Since the Old Testament speaks interchangeably of "Son," "Jacob," "chosen," "Israel," and "elect," Jesus could be the symbol for all of these.

Jesus' baptism by John is an interesting problem since John had emphasized his own unworthiness compared to the one who was to follow. John's baptism of repentance, when applied to Jesus, has raised bothersome questions for many. But since there can never be a satisfactory answer to the wrong questions, by examining Jesus' baptism not as an isolated event but in the light of subsequent events, the prophetic quality of it can be more clearly understood.

In the first place, to accept a baptism of repentance is to admit that there is something fundamentally wrong with the old way of understanding life, or the old way of living it. Baptism is that which washes away the old so that the new can take its place. There does not appear to be much foundation for the idea that Jesus' baptism was a symbolic "anointing" for kingship. The real significance of Jesus' baptism is given by Mark, with the identification of Jesus as God's Son, Israel. Assuming that Jesus is, for Mark, the symbol for Israel and it is Israel that is being baptized, the baptism then takes on symbolic significance for the nation.

Mark would then be saying to his reader that Jesus was not merely a preacher from Nazareth, or even a promised Messiah come to deliver God's people—he was himself Israel, and his baptism was the symbol of the passing away of the old Israel. To be the new Israel, Israel must put away the old way of understanding her life and must be cleansed of the old and made ready for a new understanding of life, a new relationship to God and fellowman; this in the manner of the writer of the epistle to the Ephesians who says that man must put off the old nature which belongs to a former manner of life and put on the new nature, created after the likeness of God in true righteousness and holiness (Eph. 4:22 ff.).

If this interpretation is correct, the life that Jesus is portrayed as taking up in Mark's Gospel can be expected to be of an entirely different attitude and texture from the old life of Israel. Mark's very phrase "like a dove" points to the idea of a "new life," and hints at God's Spirit "hovering over the waters" as at the creation (Gen. 1:2); the dove of creation is matched by the dove dispatched by Noah from the ark. It hovered over the waters and brought Noah the olive leaf which announced the renewed possibility of new life on earth. The revolutionary quality of the new life lived by Jesus was such that even his closest companions could not comprehend it. Eventually, those who were bound to the old life irrevocably experienced the new as their own judgment and condemnation, for which they decided Jesus must pay with his life.

The Testing

Ulrich W. Mauser in his interesting book *Christ in the Wilderness* indicates that wilderness and repentance were closely related concepts in certain communities of New Testament times. Such connection of ideas seems probable among Mark's intended readers.[6] The details of Jesus' sojourn in the wilderness are firmly rooted in the wilderness wanderings of the Old Testament. The time element is concerned with the figure "forty," echoing not only the time of the exodus itself, but also Moses' forty-day stay on Mt. Sinai, as well as Elijah's wandering through the desert to Mt. Horeb. Before the re-creation following the flood, there were forty days and nights of rain. In each instance, the period connoted by "forty" marks the beginning of new life.

There is an implicit contrast between the temptation and response of Adam and that of Jesus. Adam's failure to trust the life given him by God as a "good" life is depicted by his eating of the fruit of the tree of the knowledge of good and evil. Having thereby set up his own criteria of good and evil concerning his life, he could not believe that God intended everything in his life to work together for his fulfillment. Such failure to trust God cost him the fruit of the tree of life and dominion over all things, both of which had been part of the life gift from God. If one takes seriously the Christian conviction that Jesus was truly man, then he was also faced with the temptation of a wrong understanding of the gift of life, and the temptation to use that life for self-glory rather than in the service of God. Although Mark's account of Jesus' stay in the wilderness is very brief, still he has managed to convey the outcome of Jesus' triumph over the temptation to a wrong understanding of life and a mistrust of God as its giver by stating that "he was with the wild beasts; and the angels ministered to him" (ch. 1:13). The presence of wild beasts is traditionally associated in the Old Testament with the presence of evil (Ps. 22:11 ff.; Ezek. 34:5, 8, 25), as well as with the triumph of righteousness (Job 5:22 f.; Isa. 11:6 ff.). Psalm 91:11 ff. pairs dominion over the wild beasts with the promise of service by angels. Their ministering presence can be associated also with the food from heaven, which was God's gift to Israel during her forty years in the wilderness.

As Israel's baptism in the sea was a washing away of the past and her time in the wilderness the preparation for a new life, so might Jesus' baptism and sojourn in the wilderness be interpreted. Israel had been called by God to become a "blessing to the nations," and had failed historically; so God has called a new Israel to be his instrument of service to fulfill the role old Israel denied. The head of the new Israel, Jesus, will call a remnant of twelve from the old Israel and send it to carry God's reconciling word of love to the four corners of the world.

Galilee

It was in Galilee, Mark says, that Jesus began his ministry after his sojourn in the wilderness. Galilee was a region predominantly Gentile in the period prior to the life of Jesus, and was condemned by Judea as being profane and heretical. Jewish antipathy toward Gentiles is not difficult to understand. During the time immediately prior to the life of Jesus, Israel's history had been a turbulent one. Brooding on the impossible circumstances of life under a foreign ruler, in the light of God's promises, the apocalyptists, whose writing zenith was reached a little less than two hundred years before Christ, were forced to turn to Israel's history for answers to their questions. They searched the beginning for an explanation of that toward which all events lead—the end. During this period of history, the Gentiles were fiercely hated, perhaps with more vehemence than at any other time. Delivered from foreign rule for the first time in four hundred years by the House of Maccabee, Israel in turn rebelled against its rule when it became strictly secular in character. It was to settle this internal strife that the Romans came, and stayed to rule.

Rome was just one more foreign ruler in a long list. Israel had at one time or another been at war with, or fallen under the domination of, all her neighbors—Moab,

Edom, Syria, Assyria, Babylonia—to mention only a few. It is no wonder she hated the Gentiles, a hatred that finally culminated in almost virtual suicide when in the second half of the first century A.D. she revolted against Rome.

Her antipathy toward the Gentiles was not solely political in nature. Her theological understanding was that an attack on Israel was also an attack on God. If Israel were destroyed, God would be without representation in the world. The pleas of Deutero-Isaiah and the books of Ruth and Jonah were not pleas Israel was able to take seriously. She was the victim of the Gentile domination that precipitated the books themselves. Any "gathering of the nations" became an event assigned to the last days, and eventually became an idea more or less detached from worldly life. Such a gathering could be possible only as a result of an irresistible sweep of God's hand into history, bringing an end to the present age, and in some form or other establishing his Kingdom forever, with Israel at the pinnacle of the international hierarchy.

The hope of an actual fulfillment of the great anticipations for the postexilic period had dwindled away to nothing. Restoration more and more became assigned to an unrealized future, which in the light of understanding became synonymous with "the end." This was not, of course, the only understanding in Israel, and the postexilic understanding of Israel as the suffering servant, whose task it was to be a blessing to the nations, to gather them together for God, grew up beside the idea of political elevation and racial purity. The voice of those who believed that God intended salvation for his entire creation, however, was drowned out by the voices of the Nehemiahs and the Ezras. Israel turned more and more in upon herself, pushing conciliation with the nations of the world farther and farther away.

The prophets warned Israel that her being swallowed by the Babylonians was God's judgment upon her, and she would not find release until she accepted her obligation to preach God's salvation to the enemy. The Book of Jonah declares that the greatest task assigned to her by God is to preach his salvation to that most hated of all Gentile cities, Nineveh. Her persecution by Babylonia would not come to an end until she agreed to do the task God assigned to her in his covenant.

It was into this theological climate that Jesus was born, and this orientation to which he came speaking. The two centuries prior to the advent of Jesus Christ had been dominated by the idea of the separation of "this age" from the "age to come." Mark's Jesus shared neither this mood nor this understanding, and like Amos, was prepared to take Israel's understanding and use it against her. The difference in his understanding from that of his contemporaries, even his closest companions, is marked by their continued lack of comprehension of his life and teachings as Mark depicts them. Mark's critical attitude toward the disciples in his Gospel underscores Jesus' difference of understanding.

Although Mark states that Jesus' ministry began in Galilee, to the average Jew of that time it would appear a most peculiar place for a new outbreak of God's saving activity. Such an unlikelihood is underscored in the Gospel of John, which attributes to Nathanael the remark, "Can anything good come out of Nazareth?" (John 1:46). According to Mark, Jesus came into Galilee to work and to preach, and did not turn toward Jerusalem until the week of the passion. Mark's road to Jerusalem was the last road, the road to the end. Mark would have been sympathetic to the statement by Jeremiah: "Cast up a siege mound against Jerusalem. This is the city which must be punished; there is nothing but oppression within her" (Jer. 6:6).

The Gospel of Matthew supports Jesus' ministry in Galilee with a reference to Isa. 9:1, and Matthew refers

to the district as "Galilee of the Gentiles," which means
the same thing as Isaiah's "Galilee of the nations." Even
during Old Testament times the population of this region
was greatly mixed, and it became even more so after the
downfall of the Northern Kingdom. The name "Galilee
of the Gentiles" was originally applied to the northern
border of Israel, fenced in and permeated from three sides
by Gentiles, but gradually the area covered by the name
spread to the south. Although predominantly Gentile in
Maccabean times, the Jews began to return to it, and it
was loyal to the Jewish state during the conflicts that occurred about 4–1 B.C., so that the Gentile portion of the
name gradually dropped into misuse. Galilee was under
Jewish "law" for only about a hundred years before Christ,
however, and its customs were not scrupulously faithful
to the law. New ideas had much less difficulty being
accepted there than in the orthodox south. Judea felt
about Galilee very much the same as Israel, symbolized
by Jonah, felt about Nineveh. "Galilee itself . . . was regarded with disfavor by strict jewish piety at Jerusalem,
owing to the strong strain of gentile elements in its population and the consequent infiltration of greek ideas and
ways of life."[7] So it was in Galilee of the Gentiles that
Jesus answered his call to preach God's word. The Talmud
did not even allow the teaching of the Torah to Gentiles.
It was necessary to become a Jew before one could hear
the word of God as Israel knew it.

According to Mark, the gospel was never proclaimed in
Jerusalem or elsewhere than Galilee and its surrounding
neighbors. There was no act of power, other than the
cursing and subsequent withering of the fig tree, which
took place in Jerusalem. Jesus was hailed as king in the
triumphal entry only by those who followed him from
Galilee, and Jerusalem was portrayed as the scene of
destruction and death. Galilee and Jerusalem stand against
each other in Mark. Jerusalem was traditionally regarded

as the sacred city, the home of Jewish piety and patriotism, but Mark regarded it as a center of hostility and sin. It was to Galilee that Mark's Jesus brought the revelation of God's redeeming love.

The Preaching

Jesus began to preach in the manner of John, who was now gone, having been arrested previous to Jesus' ministry in Galilee. "The time is fulfilled, and the kingdom of God is at hand; repent, and believe in the gospel." (Mark 1:15.) Thus began the fulfillment of the prophecy of Isaiah, the beginning of a new exodus (Isa. 9:1). Throughout her history Israel had been waiting for "the time" to be fulfilled, the time when God would dwell in Zion, the holy mountain, and Jerusalem, the Holy City of Israel, would not harbor strangers; the time when God would cover her enemies with shame, and Israel would gloat over them and tread them down like mire in the streets (Micah 7:10). The time appeared to be less and less a historic possibility, and became assigned to some transcendent future; yet, Christ came preaching, "The time *is* fulfilled." To a nation in bondage to Rome, treated as little better than slaves, completely bereft of honor and prestige, with no earthly hope of being able to crush her enemies, the preaching must have seemed strange indeed. Jesus never preached that the time was *coming;* it had arrived.

Israel's acceptance of this preaching would mean the abrogation of her understanding of "the time." When Jesus called Israel to repentance, he was in effect telling her that she had all along been wrong about the time. She had always believed it to be the wrong time, or rather, not the right time. The right time seemed always to lie either in her past or somewhere in the future. To declare that the time had come was to pour new content into the old idea of "the time."

Jesus came saying the time is *now,* but then throughout Israel's history, in the light of God's call, the time had always been present. Israel had looked for salvation in the external circumstances of the world. She had looked for a sign, and Jesus told her there would be no sign. She had been given, with her life, all the sign there would ever be (Gen. 12:2)—the confrontation by her neighbors and her ministry to them as the service of God. There would be no magic, no other time—fulfillment of God's call to service must be *now.*

Chapter 2

ISRAEL IS SICK

Mark 1:16 to 2:12

Called from the Sea

GOD HAD BATTLED the sea from the beginning, when from its chaos and darkness he called forth his creation. He tamed the water with bars and doors, and said, "Thus far shall you come, and no farther" (Job 38:11). The backdrop for Mark's Gospel is the Sea of Galilee. On its shores and on its surface the drama of the life and ministry of Jesus Christ is played out.

Mark's introduction to Jesus' ministry gives way to action by the sea, where as Jesus passed along he saw two men at work. They were called and they followed. Shortly, Simon and Andrew were joined by James and John, who left their father mending nets in his boat. So the first few of the Twelve were called away from the sea to follow Jesus. Traditionally the sea was regarded as a place of death, a place to be feared, a place from which man stood in need of deliverance by God. It was more than dangerous; in the Hebrew mind it was a personalized enemy of man which would reclaim the earth if God had not set the bounds for it. So much was this so that we read in Revelation that the creation of a new heaven and a new earth was to be the time when "the sea was no more" (Rev. 21:1).

Galilee, however small, was subject to sudden terrifying squalls which tumbled across its face from the surrounding hills. Those who were fishermen on that sea would have known that death could claim them in its stormy treachery. In every respect it could qualify as a place of danger, the jaws of death. Thus, when Mark tells his reader that the first four of Jesus' followers were called away from its shore, they were symbolically being called away from primordial danger, from death. God's deliverance of Israel from Egypt had been across a sea the people feared would claim their lives. The calling of the new Israel to covenant in a new exodus takes place with the Sea of Galilee at its center. So much time in the Gospel is spent in the boat on the water that it was perhaps Mark's idea to suggest that the boat was the ark of salvation for those who followed Jesus, and that Jesus himself was the new Noah, bringing a new covenant to the chosen. The sea itself is Mark's symbol of darkness and death, and indeed, is even used by him in one instance as the scene of the reenactment of the exodus itself, to be discussed later (Mark 5:1 ff.; see Chapter 4).

Why a New Israel?

Since it is actually what came about, there is a tendency to take for granted that the split between Judaism and Christianity was a certainty from the beginning, and the Christian church was the intended event growing out of the advent of Christ. Mark does not write as if Jesus were creating something entirely different and new, but as if he was really creating a new Israel with a remnant from the old as its core. Paul's life is perhaps a good illustration of the attitude a Jew would have concerning the necessity for a new Israel. He was so fanatically attached to its traditional form, and so incensed by the followers of Christ who claimed to have become the embodiment of the fulfillment of Old Testament Scripture, that he, in a frenzy of zeal, attempted to wipe out the movement entirely. It was only when the "light" of God's truth dawned on Saul of Tarsus on the Damascus road that he knew himself as one who had been blind, one who had eyes to see and saw not.

The calling of a new Israel would be a judgment of the old Israel, of her failure to live her life in accordance with God's will. It would be admitting that a new Israel was necessary because the old Israel was sick beyond healing. As Mark continues, he begins to make clear, not only the authority and power that he believed had been given to Jesus for the calling of a new Israel, but something of the sickness that was the plague of the old.

The Unclean Spirit in the Synagogue

Jesus began teaching among his own people, and for the most part, his early ministry took place in their synagogues. Paul later declared that the word of God must be spoken first to the Jews (Acts 13:46 f.). On the Sabbath, Jesus and the four who had been called to follow him went into the synagogue, and Jesus began to teach. The astonishment expressed by the congregation at Jesus' authoritative teaching should not be unexpected. The voice of authority had not fallen on Israel's ears for a long time. The scribes taught the law to the people by reading it and the commentary on it, and Mark says Jesus did not teach as they did. As Jesus spoke, Mark says, "And immediately there was in their synagogue a man with an unclean spirit" (ch. 1:23). From whence he came, we do not know. Who he might have been is not hinted. Even the fact that he was there at all is highly puzzling, since those who were unclean were banished from corporate worship and the community, until such time as the necessary sin offering and atonement ceremony had been accomplished in their behalf. Mark says only that he appeared *immediately* after Jesus began to teach with authority and not as the scribes. Even the content of Jesus' teaching is withheld. Attention is concentrated, instead, on the fact that whatever it concerned, it prompted the revelation of the presence of an unclean spirit in the synagogue.

The primitive significance of clean and unclean was a purely ceremonial one. The prereligious understanding was that "unclean" was a form of "taboo," which could be understood in either a positive or a negative sense. For example, blood could make unclean, but when properly handled could also cleanse. Sacrificial ritual was practiced to please the "good demons," while cathartic ritual was practiced for the purpose of expelling "evil demons." That which was clean was simply *not* taboo, and contained no ceremonial taint. Purification was the removal of ceremonial taint.

Old Testament law states that uncleanness disqualified one for divine worship and sacrifice, and religious offices could not be performed in an unclean place, i.e., outside of Palestine. There were five categories of uncleanness: sexual impurity; blood; certain foods (which were either inherently unclean, such as swine, or rendered unclean by their association with idols); uncleanness connected with death (a bone or a grave transferred uncleanness, a murderer defiled the land, and even the kinsmen of the dead were rendered unclean); and, of course, leprosy, which rendered one unclean, and the healing of which had to be followed by a ceremony before the leper could be pronounced clean by the priest. The one thing about uncleanness that is of paramount importance in a discussion of Mark's Gospel is that a state of uncleanness resulting from any cause made one unable to worship God and signified a condition of sin in the individual, a blemished relationship between one and God.

The Levitical consideration of uncleanness does not make any distinction between one's broken relationship to

God, whether resulting from sin or uncleanness. The first mention of uncleanness in Leviticus occurs in ch. 5, and subsequently uncleanness is regarded as sin in the individual, for which atonement for one's guilt must be made. Uncleanness automatically established a person's guilt and precipitated his being cut off, not only from God, but also from his fellowman, because it was a condition that was transferable. Until the proper sin offering had been brought, and the priest had made atonement for the sin signified by the uncleanness, one remained unclean.

In the passage under consideration, Mark states that there was an unclean spirit (breath) loose in the synagogue. An unclean spirit would be an unholy breath, one which blew itself against God. The spirit cried out to Jesus: "What have you to do with us, Jesus of Nazareth? Have you come to destroy us? [Or, alternatively, 'You have come to destroy us.'[8]] I know who you are, the Holy One of God" (ch. 1:24).

The title "the Holy One of God" is the central issue in an episode related in the book of Numbers. There was a contest between two opposing spirits among the Hebrews in the wilderness, and the outcome was to determine who should be called "the Holy One of God" and therefore the rightful leader of the people.

A group of dissenters gathered under the leadership of Korah, the Levite, and assembled against Moses and Aaron because they had exalted themselves above the people of Israel as leaders. Although a number of different families were involved in the dispute described, the episode actually resolved itself into a struggle between the Levites and Aaron.

Aaron and his sons comprised the priesthood. The first chapter of the book of Numbers, in which the twelve tribes of the Hebrews are counted, and in which Levi, as the thirteenth tribe, is named but not counted, tells that the

Levites had been appointed by God to oversee and carry out the menial labor connected with the Tabernacle and its furnishings. They were responsible for moving the Tabernacle from one place to another, and when Israel set up camp, they were to camp immediately around it. The other Israelites were forbidden to come near, but were to pitch their tents by tribes, three to each of the four sides of the Tabernacle. The dedication of the tribe of Levi, whose service was given to Aaron by God, was one that symbolized the dedication of the firstborn of Israel, who had been consecrated as God's own (Num. 3:9 ff.). The tribe of Levi was a substitute for the firstborn of Israel.

Aaron and his sons constituted the priesthood. Moses and Aaron were, to be sure, themselves members of the tribe of Levi, but it was only Aaron and his sons who were to serve as priests (Ex. 28:1). As a matter of practice, however, the Bible speaks of the "Levitical priesthood"; and the Levites, before the fall of Jerusalem, 587–586 B.C., acted as priests. The scribes of the New Testament were probably all members of the tribe of Levi.

The rebels assembled a congregation against Moses and Aaron. Korah was jealous of Aaron, who was a Levite of the same family and only his equal in rank, and felt he should not be the chief priest for all of Israel. He was joined in the group by certain members of the tribe of Reuben, who as true firstborn of Jacob, felt that the Reubenites should have the place occupied by the Levites. The presence of this unholy spirit among the people was accepted as a challenge by Moses, who declared God would answer it himself, and Moses proposed a test for the following day. "Do this: take censers, Korah and all his company; put fire in them and put incense upon them before the LORD tomorrow, and the man whom the LORD chooses shall be *the holy one. You have gone too far, sons of Levi!*" (Num. 16:6 f., italics ours.)

When the people gathered at the appointed time, God threatened to wipe out the entire congregation, saving only Moses and Aaron. The congregation repented of their wrong spirit and prayed to the "God of the spirits of all flesh" to forgive them. They were told to separate themselves from the dwellings of Korah, Dathan, and Abiram (the latter two were members of the tribe of Zebulun). Moses told the repentant congregation to move completely away from the tents of the wicked, and they were warned not to *touch* anything belonging to the wicked. There is no specific reference concerning Korah's having an "unclean" spirit, one that prevented his properly worshiping God, but it would appear from the manner in which his sin was treated that that is exactly what he did have, and that it, like all uncleanness, was transferable. Otherwise, there seems no reason to warn the congregation to stay away from him and his possessions lest they die.

After the congregation had moved to safety, Moses said to them:

> "Hereby you shall know that the LORD has sent me to do all these works, and that it has not been of my own accord. If these men die the common death of all men, or if they are visited by the fate of all men, then the LORD has not sent me. But if the LORD creates something new, and the ground opens its mouth, and swallows them up, with all that belongs to them, and they go down alive into Sheol, then you shall know that these men have despised the LORD."

> And as he finished speaking all these words, the ground under them split asunder; and the earth opened its mouth and swallowed them up.

> (Num. 16:28 ff.)

When Jesus was confronted by the unclean spirit in the place of congregation, that is, the synagogue, he rebuked it, saying, "Be silent, and come out of him!" (Mark 1:25). All who were gathered there were amazed and exclaimed: "What is this? *A new teaching!* With authority he commands even the unclean spirits, and they obey him." (V. 27, italics ours.) As the unclean spirit embodied in the company of Korah and his followers was removed from the midst of the congregation by a *new* thing done by the Lord, and the people were left in no doubt as to whom God had chosen as the "holy one" to lead the people, so the unclean spirit vanished from the congregation surrounding Jesus before a *new* teaching.

The striking resemblance of language in the two stories presents a classic example of Mark's ability to relate his material to the Old Testament. Examination of the elements of the two stories reveals that they tell very nearly the same story, even though the people involved are in many ways very different. But it seems apparent that Mark is inferring that there is a contest beginning between Jesus, as God's chosen leader of the people, and the Levites, who were the spiritual guardians of the religious life of Israel, in much the same manner as the struggle developed between Moses and Aaron and the Levites. As Aaron was revealed as the choice of God as the "holy one," so Jesus was addressed and recognized by the unclean spirit which gave way before his command. Perhaps one of the most striking features of the Old Testament story is the statement by Moses, "You have gone too far, sons of Levi!" In the light of the development of Mark's Gospel, it would appear to be his intention to bring this to his readers' attention; i.e., the Levites, as spiritual leaders of Israel, had gone too far in their unholy attitude. Mark's Jesus has entered a contest with the Levites as to which spirit God will acknowledge as *his* spirit.

It seems consistent with Mark's style that he has used this exorcism to tell us something of the nature of Jesus from the Old Testament story concerning his authority and the necessity of calling a new Israel into being. Mark was not writing a biography, but a Gospel, a message of good news, and it appears that he does not allow the accidents of history to jeopardize his account of the meaning of the gospel. Out of whatever material he had at his disposal, and there must have been an abundance, he has chosen only that which suited his purposes, and arranged it in a manner to tell what he regarded as the true meaning of the life of Jesus Christ for the world. If he took considerable liberty with the historical sequence of events, as even someone as early as Papias has pointed out, it was because he had in mind something vastly different as his design.

Mark's choice of material alone stemmed from an arbitrary purpose. That there are healing narratives involving twelve Jews and one Gentile in Mark's Gospel is certainly no accident. (Luke has just doubled the number to twenty-six, twenty-four Jewish, two Gentile.) The choice, and even the sequential arrangement of the thirteen healing incidents, was dictated by the purpose of explaining that Jesus Christ was the fulfillment of all the Old Testament prophecies and hopes.[9]

Mark implies in his first healing narrative that there was an unclean spirit in Israel, which placed her under God's judgment and in a state of sin. As long as Israel, under the leadership of the Levites, was concerned to regard herself as the one who should be the leader of the nations of the world, instead of the servant of God ministering to those nations, then her uncleanness of spirit resulted in a broken relationship to God and cut her off from the community of the living.

In his very first healing narrative Mark has called his reader's attention to the central conflict in Jesus' ministry. The contrast between Jesus' understanding of Israel's intended relationship to God and the world and that of orthodox Judaism becomes the unifying theme of the

Gospel. The conflict deepens in intensity as the Gospel progresses. Mark is concerned here with more than an unclean spirit in a mere individual—this is a sickness in Israel itself, which must come under the healing spirit of Jesus Christ if she is to be restored to her whole relationship to God and serve him as he intended.

Simon's Mother-in-Law

When the four, with Jesus, left the synagogue and entered the house of Simon, Mark says Jesus was informed that a relative of Simon's, his mother-in-law, lay sick in her bed with a fever. Jesus came to her and took her by the hand and lifted her up.

The introduction of "fever" into the Gospel raises the question concerning Mark's choice of the specific healing narratives he uses. At the surface level, there appears to be no particular significance about the types of diseases that he emphasizes, but a more careful examination will reveal a direct relationship to the Old Testament. A list of the diseases with which he was concerned would read like this: unclean spirits, fever, leprosy, paralysis, withered hand, hemorrhage (unclean), condition that appears to be death, deafness, dumb tongue, and blindness. Some of these are duplicated to complete the list to thirteen.

The list bears a direct relationship to the prophecy of Isaiah concerning the great day of deliverance by God of the remnant from Babylon. God will make a path for his people, who under his healing hand can no longer say, "I am sick" (Isa. 33:24); "Not *one* of these shall be missing" (ch. 34:16, italics ours), for God will:

> Strengthen the weak hands,
>   and make firm the feeble knees.
>
> . . . .
>
> Then the eyes of the blind shall be opened,
>   and the ears of the deaf unstopped;

> then shall the lame man leap like a hart,
>   and the tongue of the dumb sing for joy.
>
> . . . .
>
> And a highway shall be there,
>   and it shall be called the Holy Way;
> the unclean shall not pass over it,
>
> . . . .
>
>   but the redeemed shall walk there.
> And the ransomed of the LORD shall return.
>   (Isa. 35:3, 5 f., 8–10.)

The relationship between the diseases listed in Isaiah and those in the healing narratives in Mark is immediately evident. The constitution of the remnant called by God to be his people under the leadership of Jesus, the Holy One of God, conforms to the pattern given by Isaiah. There are only two infirmities that require interpretation: the weak hands and the feeble knees. The withered hand of Mark 3:1 is Mark's "weak hand," and for any who have suffered from a fever, there will be little difficulty remembering its greatest resulting debility as a case of wobbly or feeble knees. When God calls his chosen people to exodus, he heals. His Spirit alone is that which makes people whole, which cleanses, restores, and results in new life. When Israel was called out of Egypt, she fell under God's healing hand, "for I am the LORD, your healer" (Ex. 15:26).

Simon's mother-in-law suffered from a fever. There is only one other mention of fever, per se, in the Bible, and that is in Lev., ch. 26:

> I am the LORD your God, who brought you forth out of the land of Egypt, that you should not be their slaves; and I have broken the bars of your yoke and made you walk erect.
>
> But if you will not hearken to me, and will not do all these commandments, if you spurn my statutes, and if

your soul abhors my ordinances, so that you will not do
all my commandments, but break my covenant, I will
do this to you: I will appoint over you sudden terror,
consumption, and fever that waste the eyes and cause
life to pine away. And you shall sow your seed in vain,
for your enemies shall eat it.

(Vs. 13 ff.)

Again, a healing narrative in the Gospel lends itself to
a broader interpretation than the mere healing of an individual. Fever, according to the Old Testament passage,
results from God's judgment. It is the punishment for
breaking the covenant, and its results are an inability to
walk erect, an ability that God had given to Israel when he
called her out of Egypt. Simon's mother-in-law becomes
more than simply that. She becomes the symbol for Israel,
suffering from God's judgment, lying ill with a fever that
has weakened her legs so that she cannot rise and serve.
Who can raise her up? "Fallen, no more to rise, is the
virgin Israel; forsaken on her land, with none to raise her
up." (Amos 5:2.) "There is none to guide her among all
the sons she has borne; there is none to take her by the
hand among all the sons she has brought up." (Isa.
51:18.) And in a strictly literal sense, it was not a son
of Simon's mother-in-law who raised her, it was another.
"And he came and took her by the hand and lifted her up,
and the fever left her; and she served them." (Mark
1:31.)

It is Israel herself who cannot walk, stricken with a
fever sent her because she has broken her covenant with
God, and the only one who can raise her up to serve is
this son who takes her by the hand, breathing his spirit
into her. Israel, who has been afflicted with knees too
feeble to walk in God's wide world, must rise to her feet
and serve.

Simon's house became a sort of headquarters for Jesus'
ministry. It was in Capernaum, which was perhaps located

on the northwest shore of the Sea of Galilee, and it became the cradle of the infant movement that grew into the Christian church. To Simon's house that evening, following the healing in the synagogue, came the multitude of the city—the whole city, Mark says—bringing their sick ones, afflicted in body and spirit. Mark's Jesus silenced the demons that they might not make known who he was, for the time had not yet come for that revelation.[10]

The Withdrawals

Jesus left Capernaum before dawn the following day for solitude and prayer. Mark details three specific withdrawal episodes in the first half of his Gospel. In order to understand the first, it seems necessary to deal with all the withdrawals at this point. This first time (ch. 1:35), it was only the disciples who followed him, although it is obvious that they were spokesmen for the crowd. The second withdrawal (v. 45) comes at a time when Jesus was no longer able to enter a town, and even though he withdrew to the country, people came to him from every quarter. In the third withdrawal incident (ch. 6:31) Jesus and the disciples were preceded by the crowd. They are present to meet him on his arrival.

Each withdrawal followed some strenuous activity of healing or preaching, either on the part of Jesus, or as in ch. 6, on the part of the disciples, who had just returned from their missionary journey. Each evidences an increasing popularity, so that the crowds not only precede Jesus to the place of withdrawal, but as in ch. 6, stay with him so long they become hungry.

Mark says no more of Jesus withdrawing, after his feeding narratives, until the last week in Jerusalem. When he goes apart with the disciples to Gethsemane, there are no following crowds. Not only are there no crowds, but on three separate occasions, Jesus withdrew from the disciples in order to pray, and upon returning to them three times found them sleeping. At the end, even the disciples are not with him. It is as if Mark were repeating the earlier three withdrawal episodes, only with opposite results which mark the end of Jesus' ministry, for he stated: "Are you still sleeping and taking your rest? It is enough; the hour has come; the Son of man is betrayed into the hands of sinners. Rise, let us be going; see, my betrayer is at hand" (ch. 14:41).

The Leper

After leaving Simon's house at Capernaum, Jesus did not immediately return there but went on, according to Mark, to preach and heal throughout Galilee. During this time a leper approached him, and kneeling before him said, "If you will, you can make me clean" (ch. 1:40). Leprosy rendered one unclean, officially so following a pronouncement by the priest. Such a pronouncement sentenced one to automatic expulsion from the community, and the behavior of the leper was specifically circumscribed by Old Testament law. He was required to wear torn clothes, let his hair hang loose, cover his upper lip, and cry, "Unclean, unclean." As long as he was so afflicted, he was required to live outside the community (Lev. 13:45 f.). It was the priest's duty not only to pronounce a person unclean or clean but to initiate and carry out the ceremonial ritual of cleansing required for his reinstatement as a member of the community when leprosy was found to have left him.

There is no suggestion in Leviticus that the priest had anything to do with the actual healing of leprosy. Power over leprosy belonged to God alone. In Exodus it became a sign of God's authentication of Moses, that Israel might believe that the Lord was the one who had sent him to lead the deliverance from Egypt (Ex. 4:6 f.). In Numbers, the sign of leprosy given to Miriam as a punishment for her rebellion against Moses, and her subsequent healing, were the evidence of God's power (Num. 12:9 ff.). In II Kings 5:7 ff., when Naaman's master sent him to the king of Israel to cure his leprosy, the king cried in dismay, "Am I God, to kill and to make alive, that this man sends word to me to cure a man of his leprosy?" It was the power of God, working through Elisha, which cured the man.

The leper, in Mark, had not asked to be healed of his leprosy. He had stated that Jesus could make him clean if he so desired; i.e., Jesus had the power to restore the man's broken relationship to God which was evidenced by his leprosy. The Levitical passages concerning leprosy, however, state very clearly that healing must *precede* the cleansing ceremony that restored one to the community. Jesus responded to the supplication with, "I will; be clean" (Mark 1:41). Mark states that Jesus did so in anger, although the RSV translation of Mark, and most other translations of the text, read either that he responded with pity or compassion. The most ancient texts of Mark that are available, however, state that he was moved with anger. Because it evidently presented an obstacle to think of Jesus as being angry with the supplicant, it is easy to see why an early copyist might have changed the word (and, thereby, the underlying sentiment) "anger" to "pity," but difficult to imagine the reverse. Despite what one might believe was uncharacteristic of Jesus, it is more probable that the original Marcan reading was "being angry."

Most scholars agree that this is the case,[11] which leaves us with Jesus' emotional state as one of anger, and his answer said in effect to the man, "I want to, now be clean." In addition to being angry and treating the case of leprosy, not from the standpoint of healing a disease but as cleansing a sinner, Jesus broke the law when he touched the leper. If the same interpretative technique as that used in the two previous healing narratives is applied to this incident, it begins to be clear why Jesus was angry.

If this man is a symbol for a sick Israel, then Jesus does indeed have cause to be angry. It appears that it is not so much Mark's intention to imply that Israel actually had leprosy, as it is to show that Israel lived as a leper. She lived the life that was imposed on a leper. A leper was unable to worship God because his uncleanness was a sign of God's judgment for sin, and he was not allowed near the place of worship. He was cut off from the world of the living and shut outside the community of men. Was not this Israel's historical dilemma? Had she not, because of her aloofness from the nations of the world, lived her life alone as much as possible, isolating herself from the community of the living? She had cried, "Unclean, unclean," but her cries had been directed toward the world, when it was her own spirit that was unclean. Her understanding of her covenant relationship to God and his creation was permeated by an unclean spirit which kept her from being God's servant who calls all men to him.

When the passage is interpreted in this manner, it becomes easy to understand why Mark has said that Jesus was angry when confronted by the leper, but that in spite of his anger he was willing to remove the uncleanness. He would have removed Israel's uncleanness by whatever power given to him, if only she would allow him to do so. It was his understanding of God's call, his clean (holy) spirit, which was the one element capable of cleansing Israel; but his spirit was not one that Israel would accept—she preferred her dwelling place isolated from the nations.

When Mark's Jesus stretched out his hand and touched the leper, saying, "I will, be clean," the leprosy left him, although, according to Levitical law, leprosy must leave the person before he can be pronounced clean. Jesus sent him away, angrily charging him to say nothing to anyone. However, Jesus went on to say, "But go, show yourself to the priest, and offer for your [actual] cleansing what Moses commanded, for a proof to the people" (ch. 1:44). (Since there is no English equivalent of the word for "cleansing" which appears in the Greek text, it is necessary to qualify the word "cleansing" with "actual," because the Greek word means the *actual* cleansing that has taken place, and not one which is to be the result of the customary Levitical atonement ceremony.[12]) With this in mind, it is apparent that Jesus' instructions to the man are incompatible with the Levitical passages concerning leprosy. It also appears that Jesus has contradicted his desire for secrecy. First, the man is to say nothing, and then he is to use his actual cleansing as a testimony to the people; it does not seem possible that both of these commands can be fulfilled.

First, consideration will be turned to the problem encountered with the law of Leviticus. When a person ceased to have physical evidence of the presence of leprosy (Old Testament usage of the term covered many skin eruptions, but did not include leprosy as the disease now bearing that label, which was not introduced into Palestine until New Testament times), he was to show himself to the priest. Whether or not the ceremony necessary for making one clean took place depended on the findings of the priest. If the victim appeared to be free of the disease, he was then authorized to bring to the priest a "sin offering" of oil and grain/animals, commensurate with his economic resources, to be used by the priest in a lengthy, complicated ritual, which itself results in the victim's cleansing. The "sin offering" in Mark, however, is one to be taken to the priest for a cleansing that *had already been accomplished,* and it must, therefore, be understood more in the light of a "thank offering" to God.

That there is, and has been, a long-standing difficulty in understanding the Marcan passage is given further support by turning to Matthew and Luke. Luke changed the wording of the command to read, "Make an offering for your cleansing, as Moses commanded, for a proof to the people" (Luke 5:14); and Matthew has eliminated the difficulty inherent in the instruction to make an offering for an already accomplished cleansing by saying, "Offer the gift that Moses commanded, for a proof to the people" (Matt. 8:4), thereby eliminating altogether the word meaning "actual cleansing." Both Matthew and Luke have eliminated any statement concerning the emotional state of Jesus.

It is difficult to believe that Mark was unaware of the apparent contradiction concerning the charge to secrecy. If the cleansing was to be a testimony to the people, then it could scarcely remain secret. Leprosy, and its removal, was one of the Old Testament signs to the Israelites in Egypt that Moses was the authentic representative of God, that the people "may believe that the LORD, the God of their fathers, the God of Abraham, the God of Isaac, and the God of Jacob, has appeared to you" (Ex. 4:5). It was a sign given to Moses by God when Moses protested that the people would not believe or listen to his voice. It was a sign for a people who would not heed words, who had ears to hear but would not. In Mark, leprosy, and its removal, becomes a sign to a people to accept Jesus as the authentic representative of God, sent as the leader to call them to repentance and service.

The Paralytic

Following the incident, Mark says that Jesus' popularity increased to the point where he could no longer enter a town. It was some days later that he returned to Capernaum, and the report circulated that he had returned home. So many came to listen to his preaching, Mark says, that there was no longer any room at all, and the door itself was blocked so that none could enter. Four men came carrying a paralytic to him. When they could not get near him, they took the afflicted man up on the roof, where, Mark says, they literally "dug a hole" (in the roof) and lowered the man into it and the helpless man's pallet came to rest in front of Jesus.

The suggestion is very strong that this man was like one dead, carried by four, reminiscent of pallbearers, and lowered into a hole prepared to receive him, as in burial. Jesus was touched by the faith of those who brought him, believing that he could restore this man to the living. When he perceived their faith, he said, "My son, your sins are forgiven" (Mark 2:5). There was immediate reaction to his words among the scribes present, and Mark says they questioned in their hearts and accused him of blasphemy, although apparently in silence. God alone is able to forgive sins—why did this man presume to such an office? Their opposition did not go unnoticed by Jesus, who upon perceiving it asked them why they questioned, saying, "Which is easier, to say to the paralytic, 'Your sins are forgiven,' or to say, 'Rise, take up your pallet and walk'?" (v. 9).

Indeed, which was easier for God when confronted by the disobedient spirit of Israel, to say "Your sins are forgiven" or "Pick up your pallet and walk?" *Walk* was the one thing she was most unwilling to do. She, like Jonah, would walk only one day's journey into a Gentile city that was three days' in breadth, and then every step of the way under protest. "Arise, go to Nineveh, that great city, and cry against it," God had commanded Jonah, the symbol for Israel. When Jonah refused to obey, he was swallowed up by the serpent in the sea, and when Jonah finally promised to obey, the serpent gave him up. The word of the Lord came again saying, "Arise, go to Nineveh, that great city, and proclaim to it the message that I tell you" (Jonah 3:2). After a desultory and reluctant fulfillment of the command, Jonah retired to the comfortable isolation of a booth (Tabernacle) and waited to see the destruction of the city. But the king of Nineveh heard the message and repented, and called upon all his subjects to repent, which caused Jonah to be furious. In essence, his angry cry to God said: "Didn't I tell you that if word got out about what a gracious, loving God you are, people would repent of their way of living and turn to you? That's why I ran away to the ends of the earth because I didn't want to tell the world, particularly that hated Gentile city, Nineveh." Jonah wished to die; he would rather have been dead than share God with the Gentile world.

No, it was not easy to say to Israel, "Rise, take up your pallet and walk," for Israel refused to walk, and her life had become like this helpless paralytic lying before Jesus, who was like one dead, ready for burying, paralyzed, i.e., unable to perform any part of the role of messenger. It would be easier to tell Israel that it was too late to be a messenger, that God had finally given up but that, nevertheless, her sins were forgiven. Jesus said to the scribes, " 'But that you may know that the Son of man has authority on earth to forgive sins'—he said to the paralytic—'I say to you, rise, take up your pallet and go home' " (Mark 2:10 f.). There was apparently no use to send the man anywhere other than home.

The Son of Man

The narrative concerning the paralytic contains the first instance of the use of the title "Son of man" as applied to Jesus. It appears to be one that, in Mark, Jesus himself appropriated and used. It is a title commonly associated with Daniel, who speaks of the "son of man" as the one who will have dominion over all things. Daniel recounts from a vision:

> And to him was given dominion
> and glory and kingdom,
> that all peoples, nations, and languages
> should serve him;

> his dominion is an everlasting dominion,
>   which shall not pass away,
>   and his kingdom one
>   that shall not be destroyed.
>   (Dan. 7:14.)

The term in Daniel is used as a "collective symbol" for Israel (as it also appears in Ps. 80:17), who in the last times would come into glory, her empire established, her dominion encompassing all things. In other literature, where the Son of Man is regarded as a personal messiah, his coming was one which would mean the end of the heathen empires and the establishment of the Kingdom of God, and through him Israel would be purified and glorified. Because of him, all who dwell on earth would recognize and praise God, and his coming would culminate in the salvation of the righteous and the judgment, condemnation, and destruction of the wicked. Never again would Israel suffer defeat at the hands of her enemies—she would become and remain victorious. Because of the seeming impossibility of such an event taking place in history, gradually the fulfillment was assigned to a time at the end of time and given a posthistorical setting.

In view of the contrasting opinions previously noted between Mark's Jesus and Israel concerning her role and her life, it seems unlikely that they would have shared an understanding of the day of the Son of Man, but not impossible that Mark may have used the term very much in the same manner in which Amos used the concept of the "day of the LORD" in a way quite contrary to popular understanding.

Sigmund Mowinckel in his book *He That Cometh* agrees that Jesus did not associate himself with the traditional and popular expectations of the Jews concerning the Messiah. Mowinckel quotes Toynbee's idea that "Jesus came to be, not the Messiah, but the Son of Man."[13] He enlarges on this point, saying that a crucified messiah defeats the idea of a Jewish messiah. He points out that Jesus' use of the term did not necessarily limit the meaning of it to a linkage between himself and man or humanity, but that as a man during his earthly ministry, he has also the powers of the Kingdom of God within. He has power over the elements, is Lord of the Sabbath, and will one day be exalted to heaven to sit at God's right hand. Mowinckel states that Jesus, as depicted in the Gospels, has included an additional element into the concept of the Son of Man, and that is the role of the Suffering Servant. He states that the death of the Son of Man, who is also the Servant, adds a new dimension to the role of Christ, and creates a new possibility that "the many" might be saved.[14]

It does not seem that Mark has used the term "Son of man" in the way in which it is used in Ezekiel, where the term simply means "mortal." The Hebrew root of the term means *ben-Adam,* or the "son of Adam." Adam is Hebrew for "everyman," and if we think of Jesus referring to himself literally as the "son of Adam," then any reference to his authority takes on a twofold significance. One of the clearest concepts of Dan., ch. 7, is that the Son of Man will be given dominion over all things, but then Gen., ch. 1, states that from the beginning this was God's intention for his creatures. "Then God said, 'Let us make man in our image, after our likeness; and let them have dominion over the fish of the sea, and over the birds of the air, and over the cattle, and over all the earth, and over every creeping thing that creeps upon the earth.' " (Gen. 1:26.)

Neither Genesis nor Daniel states that Adam or the Son of Man has the authority to forgive sins. With Mark's story of the paralytic, and Jesus' statement that his sin was forgiven, a new dimension to the office of the Son of Man has been revealed—the power to forgive sin, a power residing with God alone.

Summary

The three healing narratives, following the exorcism in the synagogue, are alike in one respect—Jesus did not in any of the three heal the diseases themselves, but eliminated the kind of life resulting from the diseases. Simon's mother-in-law lay ill with a fever, a disease named in the Old Testament as a sign of a broken covenant relationship with God. It was after Jesus took her by the hand and raised her up to serve that the fever left her. The leprosy disappeared when the man who sought Jesus' help was cleansed of his uncleanness, which was the manifestation in the Jewish mind that the disease resulted from a blemished relationship with God. To the paralytic, after extending him forgiveness, Jesus had said, "Arise, take up your pallet and go home," and when the command was obeyed, the man's paralysis, which Jesus indicated could be healed by restoration from sin, no longer had power over his life.

It is clear in each of the incidents that Mark's Jesus was not concerned merely with the healing of disease. In fact, at no point can he be said to have directly healed the disease involved. Each of these lives was being lived in a certain way, incapacitated for service to God and thereby incapable of fulfillment. In each case, including the exorcism in the synagogue, Mark indicates that underlying the apparent affliction was a broken relationship with God, and thus, in Mark, Jesus is portrayed not so much as a miraculous healer as he is as the agent of God's forgiveness and reconciling love.

The line of interpretation suggested, that is, that when Mark related these healing incidents he had Israel in mind and not merely the individuals concerned, removes most of the dilemmas created by individualizing them and treating them as details in a biographical or ordinary historical account. If the healing narratives are taken individually, i.e., as a mere unrelated collection of healing stories, it becomes difficult to understand either the reactions Mark attributes to Jesus or the specific manner in which the healings are narrated by Mark. The presupposition that Mark was only writing "history" conceals his symbolic meaning, and indeed, confronts one with numerous details that must somehow be "explained away."

The problems facing the interpreter of Mark are manifold. A Jew would have been horrified to discover the presence of a person with an *unclean* spirit in his synagogue, a fact known in the abstract by every Biblical scholar, yet it is strange that this fact excites so little attention and is generally ignored. There appears to be nothing extraordinary about the sickness of Simon's mother-in-law until one becomes aware of its Old Testament background. This background, coupled with the manner in which Mark relates the sequence of the healing, should be sufficient to indicate that more is intended here than a simple incident of healing.

The case of the leper particularly lends itself to the belief that Mark has used these healing narratives to speak of the sickness of Israel herself. There are two words in this narrative which, because they have not been understood as they appear, actually have been altered by early copyists or translators, even in the face of fairly conclusive textual evidence to the contrary. "Anger" continues to be replaced by "compassion." These two words become not only meaningful but reveal a great deal about Mark's Gospel. That Jesus would have been *angry* with *Israel* for her isolation and detachment is perfectly understandable, and that he would have *angrily* charged an Israel who had consistently refused to hear God's call to service is equally understandable. Because she would not hear, a sign was given to her to heed the authentic one from God. To translate "anger" as "compassion," it is necessary not only to second-guess Mark but to use a meaning that would ordinarily be regarded as secondary from the sources available.

This approach to the healing narratives provides an answer to another of Mark's so-called riddles when considering the story of the paralytic. The irony in Jesus' reply to the dissension of the scribes is quite evident when he asked, apparently with tongue in cheek, which was easier, to forgive Israel her sins or to tell her to arise and walk?

To the Hebrew there were no secondary causes. Scripture writers referred all things immediately to the will of God. It would not appear harsh to a Jew, therefore, to call the apparent diseases in Mark's healing narratives afflictions visited upon a people by God because they had not heard his word or kept his covenant: the very concept of "sickness" or "disease" in the Hebrew mind was just that. There are only rare exceptions where disease or sickness in the Old Testament are ascribed to any other cause than God's judgment on a rebellious, disobedient, and sinful people.

Throughout the Old Testament, disease is the manifestation of God's wrath and judgment:

> Every sickness also, and every affliction which is not recorded in the book of this law, the LORD will bring upon you, until you are destroyed. Whereas you were as the stars of heaven for multitude, you shall be left few in number; because you did not obey the voice of the LORD your God.
>
> (Deut. 28:61 f.)

Elijah pronounced God's judgment on the kings of Judah, those who had led the people after the manner of Ahab:

> Behold, the LORD will bring a great plague on your people, your children, your wives, and all your possessions, and you yourself will have a severe sickness with a dis-

ease of your bowels, until your bowels come out because
of the disease, day by day.

> (II Chron. 21:14 f.)

Deuteronomy states:

> And the generation to come, your children who rise up
> after you, and the foreigner who comes from a far land,
> would say, when they see the afflictions of that land and
> the sicknesses with which the Lord has made it sick . . .
> "Why has the Lord done thus to this land?" . . . "It is
> because they forsook the covenant of the Lord."
>
> (Deut. 29:22, 24–25.)

These passages express the typical attitude of the Old
Testament writers concerning disease. God not only judges
men and afflicts them with disease when they are disobedient, he also heals those who call on him in repentance and hearken to his word, e.g., Ex. 23:25; Deut.
7:15; Ps. 107:17 ff.

If Mark is truly reflecting the Old Testament understanding of sickness and disease, then in his healing narratives Jesus does not appear as the compassionate healer
filled with pity for a suffering people; rather, he appears
as one having God's power to forgive and restore from
sinful affliction. From an Old Testament viewpoint, God
is also the creator of woe and affliction:

> I am the Lord, and there is no other.
> I form light and create darkness,
>   I make weal and create woe,
>   I am the Lord, who do all these things.
>
> (Isa. 45:6 f.)

Both the good spirit and the evil spirit are of God: "Now
the Spirit of the Lord departed from Saul, and an evil
spirit from the Lord tormented him" (I Sam. 16:14).

Ultimately, all things issue from God and fall under his purpose.[15]

Dualism—i.e., the existence of an independent force of evil—appears to have crept into Judaism under Persian and Babylonian influence, and is found only in the post-exilic literature. It is inherent in The Book of Daniel, and there is further evidence of it in the New Testament, particularly in the book of Revelation. Later Jewish dualism, concerned with sin and the fall of man, believed that the only remedy was a new creation, and not merely a new spirit and a new heart (Jer. 31:33 ff.; Ezek. 18:31). A sweep of the divine hand must overthrow Satan.[16] Little attention is given to the "devil" in the Old Testament,[17] although his connection with the Fall is understood, and scattered throughout are references to him as the tempter of man and his tormentor. Believing in the existence of demons as servants of "Satan," or in an evil force opposing God, is to recognize dualism as a fact. Dualism is not, however, a dominant Old Testament tradition. While it does not appear to be a dominant element in the Old Testament, yet orthodox Judaism accepted the existence of good and bad spirits, and the evidence of such ideas resides in the haggada, i.e., popular lectures, which were not on the same level with the law. Rabbinic Judaism stood against dualism. The rabbis stressed that the one efficacious phylactery was the law, and the study of the law would deliver one from evil. The observance of the law was a safeguard, the panacea to evil.[18]

The early Hebrews feared few of the animistic demons or spirits, only those of the "waste places" and of the thickets beset by wild beasts. There appears to be evidence of a more developed demonology in the pseudepigraphical literature, where the influence of pagan literature is traceable.[19]

"Demon" (*daimōn*) is not an Old Testament word; that is, there are no words in the Old Testament which correspond to "demon" as it appears in the Synoptic tradition. The only instances in the Old Testament relating to demons are in references having to do with pagan worship. "Satyrs" (*sair*) are mentioned twice (Lev. 17:7; II Chron. 11:15). A satyr was a hairy one, a kid, or a goat. And twice mention is made of the worship of demons (*shed*), i.e., "spoiler" or "destroyer" (Deut. 32:17; Ps. 106:37). The idea of demon possession is not a Pauline concept, nor does the idea appear to be present in any of the other epistles, where the demon references coincide very closely with Old Testament usage concerning pagan worship. The use of the word in the Gospel of John is confined to Jesus alone, whom the people claimed had a demon; i.e., he was believed to be insane.

This leaves only the Synoptic Gospels in which the idea of being possessed by a demon or demons abruptly appears fully developed, at variance with the remainder of the Biblical tradition. Secular sources for the introduction of demon possession into the Christian tradition are of little value, for while they do point out that the concept in Judaism was taken over from both pagan and Oriental beliefs, they seem to accept the idea that a shift in Western thought about demons came about contemporaneously with the rise of Christianity. Yet, the almost complete absence of the idea, as it appears in the healing narratives of the Synoptic Gospels, in the balance of Christian literature is a puzzling one, at best.

On the other hand, the belief in demon possession as it appears in the Gospels was a very common tradition in Greek thought. Demons were believed to have plagued whole generations of particular families; illness and insanity were thus explained.[20] Mark may certainly have had some knowledge of this Greek tradition. He wrote in the Greek language and could have had some familiarity with Greek literature. It would seem not difficult to accept the idea that he had adopted the vocabulary and adapted the understanding to suit his purposes in writing, just as it is claimed that Paul changed the traditional gospel preaching language in order to express to his audience a gospel that would not be misunderstood. Jesus had preached what was interpreted as dangerous enough to warrant his crucifixion. When Paul preached to the Gentiles at Thessalonica, he was interpreted as preaching dangerously, and as meaning to incite revolution against Caesar. It is claimed by many that he altered his preaching vocabulary to preclude this kind of interpretation.[21]

Paul's preaching and writing were closer in historical time to the life of Jesus himself, while the Gospel of Mark is farther removed in time and written for a different audience. Paul preached to Gentiles in Palestine and to Greek Gentiles throughout the eastern Mediterranean countries. Mark, while he may have been Paul's protégé John Mark and would therefore have been familiar with Paul's preaching, wrote his Gospel in Rome, in the Greek language, probably as many as thirty years after the death of Christ. Paul's conversion and subsequent ministry were not separated from Christ's death by more than a few years at most.

Which tradition is prior and which changed—the understanding of the life and death of Jesus Christ which is in the Pauline tradition, or that which is portrayed by Mark and the other two Synoptic Gospels, Matthew and Luke? Indeed, is it a matter of tradition at all, or simply Mark's inventive literary imagery as contrasted to Paul's "historical" preaching? It is commonly assumed that Mark wrote out of the Christian oral tradition, and such written sources as "Q," etc., are postulated. Still, one cannot fail to question the difference between the Pauline tradition and the Synoptic Gospel tradition. The "coming of the kingdom of God," which is central in the Synoptic tradition, is practically nonexistent in Paul. Miracles had played a prominent role in the deliverance of Israel out of Egypt and the wilderness wanderings, and over 50 percent of the first ten chapters of the Gospel of Mark deal directly or indirectly with the miraculous in Jesus' ministry. Yet there are only a few references to miracles in the book of The Acts, where Paul is a major character, and there are no miracles in the preaching and writings of Paul himself.

If Mark's is, in fact, the first of the Synoptic Gospels, and the other two are based on his as is generally assumed, it should not be surprising that their accounts are patterned after Mark and utilize the same literary imagery in the healing narratives, which makes the Synoptics unique in the New Testament canon. It is not unlikely that Matthew and Luke simply took over Mark's imagery.

Whatever lay behind Mark's manner of writing, it can be said with some confidence on the basis of available information that Mark took an understanding of disease, which was traditional in Judaism, and, combining it with a belief adopted from Greek thought, devised a way of describing the visitation of God's wrath upon a people who had failed to hear his word and keep his covenant. Mark continued to do this throughout the Gospel. An individual, the symbol of Israel, suffers from the effect of an affliction resulting from a broken relationship to God. Through this symbolism, God's loving Spirit, who can forgive and restore a penitent to acceptance and health, is declared to be present in Jesus of Nazareth.

Mark has thus far indicated the anticipation of the beginning of a new exodus, relating the beginning of Jesus' ministry to the calling of the captive Israel out of bondage in Egypt. When Moses was sent to call Israel out, he was told to warn Pharaoh that failure to release the Israelites would be punished by the death of the firstborn of all Egypt. The Hebrews believed that any threat against the firstborn of a nation was in fact a threat against the entire people, for the firstborn was to them a symbol of the whole. If the firstborn of a nation were destroyed, it would be the effective destruction of the nation as a whole. It was the implementation of this threat against Egypt which finally caused Pharaoh to capitulate to Moses' demands and allow Israel to leave. If Mark is to continue using the exodus as the basic pattern of his Gospel, then one would logically expect to find him concerned with the fate of Israel's firstborn, Levi, to whom already a challenge has been issued. Levi was the symbol of Israel's firstborn, set apart by Moses as having been taken by God instead of the firstborn of all the people of Israel (Num. 8:16) and as a matter of fact, Mark takes up the matter of Levi next.

Chapter 3

THE OMISSION OF LEVI

Mark 2:13 to 3:19

Levi Is Called

JESUS RETURNED to the sea, teaching those who gathered wherever he went. Now, although it seems a strange location for a tax office, Mark says that Levi, the son of Alphaeus, was sitting at the tax office beside the sea. Levi rose and followed when Jesus said, "Follow me" (Mark 2:14).

Up until the calling of Levi, Mark has related four calling and four healing narratives. Before the final naming of the Twelve (ch. 3:13 ff.), he relates another healing narrative, which brings the total to five calling and five healing stories. The calling of a tax collector as a follower would be odious to the Jews. Tax collectors were regarded as traitors to their own people because they were Roman hirelings whose job it was to collect taxes from the Jews for the support of the Roman government. It was only the most base Jew who would have engaged in such a vocation. In addition, the tax collectors not only betrayed their own people by hiring out to Rome but cheated the people to line their own pockets in the bargain. They collected as much as the traffic would allow and pocketed the difference between their collections and that due to Rome.

The concern here is not only with the significance of the calling of a tax collector as such, but particularly with one named "Levi." Mark would have had no difficulty discovering a Levi who was a tax collector. Levi was a common enough name.

Twelve plus One

The particular case in point is the absence of "Levi" from the final list of the Twelve. There have been as many attempts to explain this omission as there have been interpreters of Mark. Comparison with the other Gospels for clarification presents even further difficulty. Matthew and Mark list a "Thaddaeus," and Luke lists an additional "Judas," the son of James. There are two "Simons" on all lists, the one in addition to Peter is identified by both Mark and Matthew as "the Cananaean," and by Luke as "the Zealot." All lists name "Philip" as the fifth name after Peter, Andrew, James, and John, where one might logically expect to find Levi. Examination of the individual calling stories in Matthew (Mark records only the five) reveals that Matthew's version of the calling of the original four, and later of the fifth, is identical except the tax collector has been named "Matthew" instead of Levi. Luke relates only one individual calling, and that is the calling of Levi, the tax collector, followed eventually by the list of the Twelve, Levi omitted.

The identification of Levi with Matthew has been widely accepted, or with James, the son of Alphaeus, but these two solutions to the problem are conjectures not supported by Mark's text,[22] which very carefully, in the list of the Twelve, indicates changed names and "nicknames." Surely, if Mark had wanted his readers to believe that Levi and Matthew were two names for the same person, he would have made this identification clear as with the others. The very fact that Luke has related no other individual callings than this one concerning Levi should indicate that there is something particularly noteworthy about it. Luke's subsequent omission of Levi from the

Twelve would likewise indicate that he understood something of Mark's intention, indeed, that he wanted to sharpen it. There is no way to know why Matthew failed to mention Levi. The fact, however, that Luke deliberately included the individual calling of Levi but mentioned no other individual callings, and then eliminated Levi from the final list, as did Mark, would seem to cast doubt on the traditional explanation that Levi is to be identified as "Matthew, the tax collector." However one resolves the versions of Matthew and Luke, our concern is with Mark's Gospel. Mark was writing no simple record of history, nor was he merely assembling (as with scissors and paste) a group of previously separate narratives. His is a mythological interpretation of the meaning of the Christ event—a Gospel.

Mark's Jesus named twelve disciples, and it is not difficult to perceive that Mark believed these Twelve were to be the new Israel, the symbolic replacement of the twelve tribes of old. Mark names thirteen disciples, if Levi and Matthew are counted separately, but Israel was composed of twelve tribes *if* you count the way the Old Testament counts. The book of Numbers (Num. 1:19) states that God commanded Moses to number the people of Israel who were gathered at the mountain of Sinai. The list of tribes as given there is as follows: Reuben, Simeon, Gad, Judah, Issachar, Zebulun, Ephraim, Manasseh, Benjamin, Dan, Asher, and Naphtali—twelve in all. At least, there are only twelve until v. 47, where it says, "But the Levites were not numbered by their ancestral tribe along with them." Named but not numbered, just like the disciples in Mark. Levi was named but not numbered among the Twelve. There were not merely twelve tribes making up Israel; there were thirteen. There is no doubt that Levi was to be considered a tribe, for Num. 1:49 states that God told Moses, "Only the tribe of Levi you shall not number." The tribe of Levi was to function as the priests of Israel, and they were not given an inheritance of land. They were appointed as overseers of the Tabernacle, the dwelling place of God in the midst of his people.

The numbering of the thirteen tribes as only twelve (they are never numbered as thirteen in the Bible) is accomplished differently in the book of Genesis. Genesis 48:5 ff. relates the adoption by Jacob of Joseph's first two sons, Manasseh and Ephraim. Jacob said, "Ephraim and Manasseh shall be mine, as Reuben and Simeon are." However, when Jacob called his sons together for the final blessing (ch. 49), Joseph appears among the twelve while Manasseh and Ephraim do not. In the list of the tribes as it appears in Numbers, and subsequent to that time, Joseph's name is coupled with Ephraim, Manasseh is listed separately, and Levi is named but not numbered.

There is a strong numerical pattern in the Gospel of Mark of twelve plus one: in the calling, healing, and feeding narratives. Mark's omission of Levi was surely intentional and deliberate, and the text immediately surrounding his calling prepares the reader for just this omission. The warning indirectly issued to the Levites in the exorcism scene in the synagogue has been brought to fruition. The spiritual leadership of the Levites is no more.

The Old and the New Law

Following Levi's call, Mark says Jesus shared a meal with tax collectors and sinners, recalling the "messianic" passage in Isaiah: "and was numbered with the transgressors; yet he bore the sin of many, and made intercession for the transgressors" (Isa. 53:12). The scribes and Pharisees complained to Jesus' disciples about the unsavory company, but when Jesus heard them he remarked that the healing which he brought was intended only for those who understood themselves to be sinners (sick). Then Jesus was criticized for failing to fast on the proper day, and his rejoinder was the question concerning whether or not wedding guests fasted when the bridegroom was with them. In the time of feasting, one does not fast. God is portrayed as the husband of his covenanted people in the Old Testament (Hos. 2:16; Isa. 54:5 f.; 62:4 f.; Ezek. 16:7 ff.). There is evidence that the idea of bridegroom as messiah had gained significance at the time of Jesus, and he is referred to as the bridegroom of the church in the New Testament.[23]

In the ensuing discussion with the scribes and Pharisees, Jesus proclaimed that the new deliverance was incapable of being incorporated into the old framework. One would not sew a piece of unshrunk cloth on an old garment, because the patch would tear away, leaving an even larger tear. One would not put new wine into old wineskins, because they would burst and the wine would be lost. New wine is for fresh skins. The old must be cast off because, by its very nature, it cannot receive and hold the new exodus. A rigid, unreforming Israel is a worn-out garment that cannot be patched up with the new cloth of the new exodus, a worn-out wineskin that is incapable of holding the new wine of understanding which Jesus brought.

Later, when Mark's Jesus and his disciples were going through the grainfields on the Sabbath, they plucked ears of corn. Then the Pharisees criticized Jesus for gathering food on the wrong day, not for eating on the wrong day as before. Clearly, Mark has deliberately depicted Jesus and the disciples as being careless with the law of the Sabbath, as well as the laws concerning fasting. The Pharisees were reminded by Jesus that David had gone even farther and set himself above the priests in the Temple when he took the showbread, and then, as a layman, distributed the bread to the laymen who were with him, even though the showbread was the special possession of the priests (I Sam.

21:1 ff.). Then Jesus said, "The sabbath was made for man, not man for the sabbath; so the Son of man is lord even of the sabbath." (Mark 2:27 f.)

Jesus has called, he has healed, he has eaten with those who were his followers; now Mark portrays him as law-giver, with his own interpretation of the law, which is contradictory to that of the scribes and the Pharisees. It is a new law. And as for the scribes and the Pharisees, religious overseers for Israel, they could not even distinguish which was more important—man's need or man's rules. The written law itself was challenged, for Ex. 31:14 states that breaking the Sabbath by doing any work was punishable by death, and even though the oral tradition had greatly modified what constituted "work," this did not weaken the challenge. There is a strong undercurrent of Paul's understanding in Mark's writing: "But now we are discharged from the law, dead to that which held us captive, so that we serve not under the old written code but in the new life of the Spirit" (Rom. 7:6; cf. also Eph. 4:22 ff.; Col. 3:9 f.; Heb. 8:13).

The Withered Hand

Again Mark says that Jesus entered the synagogue and there was there a man with a withered hand (ch. 3:1 ff.). The scribes watched to see whether or not Jesus would do further violence to the Sabbath by healing the man, in order to have additional evidence with which to accuse him. Instead of approaching the incident of healing on the Sabbath as a commission of evil, Jesus took the view that the omission of a good is a more serious breach of God's law. Mark states that he was angry with them and also grieved at their hardness of heart when they remained stubbornly silent. Here again is a reflection of the exodus story which emphasized the hardness of Pharaoh's heart. As it was hardhearted Pharaoh who held God's people in captivity then, now it is the hierarchy of Judaism whose hearts are hardened, and who are attempting to hold a people captive to the letter of the law.

The account of the withered hand points the reader to the Old Testament passage, I Kings 13:1 ff., which, it would appear, Mark has interpreted as a messianic passage. It concerns a prophet sent by God to Bethel, where he found King Jeroboam burning incense at an altar he had built. Jeroboam had built two altars and several "high places," hired his own priests to handle the sacrifices of the people, all in an effort to keep the people under his domination. The people were not, of course, supposed to sacrifice anyplace but at the Temple in Jerusalem. Jeroboam made two golden calves to which he offered sacrifices on the altar at Bethel. The man of God prophesied the destruction of both the altar and the priests. When Jeroboam stretched out his hand, saying, "Lay hold of him," his hand was "dried up," the altar was torn down, and the ashes were poured out. Jeroboam petitioned the man for restoration of his hand, and it was restored. The man was then invited to Jeroboam's house and promised a reward, but the prophet stated that not even half of Jeroboam's house could persuade him to have anything to do with him.

A reference to this story by Mark, in connection with the story of the withered hand in the synagogue, could be construed as an indirect warning issued to those who worshiped wrongly, and who led their people astray in order to keep them subject. The destruction of the altar in the Old Testament story is perhaps a veiled hint at what Mark brings out clearly in the oracle, ch. 13, i.e., the prophecy of the destruction of the Temple.

Jesus restored the withered hand of the man in the synagogue in defiance of the dissent against him for healing on the Sabbath, and the Pharisees held council with the Herodians in an effort to discover some method of destroying him. Another enemy has been added to the fold. Mark's Jesus was a threat to the established order of religion, and therefore, a threat to the Pharisees, who clung stubbornly to the *status quo*. Likewise, because of his popularity with the multitudes who stayed the hand of those seeking his destruction, he threatened political upset, and as a result, was a threat to the Herodians, defenders of Roman political power who had no desire for civil strife.

Calling the Twelve

Next, Mark states that Jesus withdrew with his disciples to the sea, and a mixed multitude followed them, one group consisting of Galileans, and one from more distant parts, including the predominantly Gentile region of Tyre and Sidon. (Cf. Ex. 12:37 f., where a "mixed multitude" went with Moses and the Israelites out of Egypt.) Jesus' popularity had grown so that it was necessary to have in readiness a boat for his protection in case the crowd should crush him, "for he had healed many, so that all who had diseases pressed upon him to touch him. And whenever the unclean spirits beheld him, they fell down before him and cried out, 'You are the Son of God.' And he strictly ordered them not to make him known." (Mark 3:10 ff.)

So far, only the reader, who was a witness at the baptism, and the unclean spirits in Israel recognize Mark's Jesus as the "Son of God." Jesus did not deny the title; he simply did not want it made known. Those outside the Kingdom of God were to be taught only in parables, so that they might see but not perceive, hear but not understand, lest they should turn again and be forgiven (ch. 4:12). Mark's Jesus, like the prophet Isaiah, was sent to a people whose eyes would be shut and ears stopped by his message, "until cities lie waste without inhabitant, and houses without men, and the land is utterly desolate" (Isa. 6:11). Mark, in ch. 13, relates that Jesus himself disclaimed to know when that time would come; only God the Father knew the time. It is evident, however, that the crowd took him, not for the kind of deliverer he was in Mark, but rather as a Davidic messiah. The popular conception of a Davidic messiah was that he would be a triumphant earthly king, who would restore Israel to riches and glory. This was not, however, the self-conscious role of Mark's Jesus.

Following his involvement with the crowds, Jesus went up to the mountain (ASV) and appointed twelve to carry on the work of Israel in the new exodus (ch. 3:13 ff.). Levi is not named. There were now only the Twelve plus Jesus. Jesus had taken the place Levi occupied in old Israel—he is the whole priesthood of the new Israel. Levi is not included in the Twelve. Why? In the Old Testament exodus, God warned Pharaoh that he would destroy the firstborn of those who held his people captive if they were not released from bondage. The firstborn of Israel was Levi, and it was the Levites, the priests, who held God's people captive to the law and tradition. The elimination of Levi, the firstborn, would, for the Hebrew mind, symbolize the destruction of Israel herself. It was not only the Jews who were held captive; the mixed multitude of the world who would hear God's word gladly (remember Nineveh) was also captive, because under the leadership of the Levitical priesthood, Israel had failed to become a blessing to the nations, refusing to share the word of God's care for the whole world, her part of the covenant with God. Levi was no longer a part of God's chosen people, and in the end, it was the chief priests who recognized Jesus, the deliverer, as their enemy, and it was they who contrived his death.

By the time Mark actually wrote, the absence of Levi from the New Israel, the Christian church, was an established fact, for the Christian movement had split from traditional Judaism. If Mark was the spokesman for Peter/Paul, he could have had no better teachers to sear into his mind the causes for that split, which were the identical causes for the conflict between Jesus and the Levites which Mark planted in his Gospel. Indeed, if Mark is John Mark of The Acts, he would have had firsthand knowledge and experience of the growing conflict and the arrest and imprisonment of the disciples by the priests for preaching Jesus Christ. (Cf. Acts 4:1 ff.; 5:17 f.; 5:27 ff.; 8:1 ff.; 15:1 ff.) The crux of the conflict was that the religious leaders then in control were unwilling to relinquish any part of the written or oral law, or accept any reinterpretation. As long as the Christians remained a part of Judaism, the traditionalists insisted that they must be circumcised and live under the law.

There is one final ironic twist to Mark's account, and that is the fact that Levi was identified as a tax collector, a career already discussed. If Levi is also to be identified as the symbol of the tribe of Levi, there was scarcely a more humiliating, insulting comparison that Mark could have made. Of all the people with whom to be identified, a tax collector would most have been anathema, for he was one whom the Jews felt had treacherously betrayed his own people—gaining his living from them, while doing so in the service of the enemy. It would appear that Mark has made just such an accusation against Levi, the priesthood.

Summary

Levi, a tax collector, was added to the list of those called by Jesus to be his followers. Jesus' association with the riffraff of society was questioned by the Pharisees, as was his nonchalance concerning the law, both written and oral. Jesus is portrayed by Mark as transcendent over the scribes and the law. The new exodus does not come under the rules of the old, which are inflexible and outgrown.

Symbolically, Mark has pointed out what happened to one who would stretch out his hand against the man of

God, Jesus. While healing would be offered, the false altars of those who plotted against Jesus to destroy him were threatened by the righteousness of God.

When Jesus went up on the mountain, the traditional gathering place of God's chosen to enter into covenant with him, he named the twelve followers for the new exodus, who are the replacement for the twelve tribes of old. Levi, who had been called, is not numbered among the Twelve. Levi, the symbol for the firstborn of Israel, has no existence in the new exodus, and his elimination is the symbol of the death of the old Israel which is replaced by the new. In Levi's place, Mark puts Jesus as the priest and leader for the new Israel.

Chapter 4

THE LITTLE EXODUS

Mark 3:20 to 5:20

Beelzebul

FOLLOWING THE CALL of the disciples at the end of ch. 3, Mark inserts a summary of what has come to pass as a result of the events that have occurred in the first three chapters. The summary is incorporated in his story of the conflict between Jesus and the scribes concerning Beelzebul, the discussion of blasphemy, and Jesus' relationship to his family. Following is a discussion of this passage interpreted in the light of Mark's mythology of the Christ event and the Old Testament references that his summary appears to consider.

The very use of the name "Beelzebul" can lead the reader to one place only in the Old Testament, even though there is a slight alteration in spelling which will be discussed later. The name appears in connection with Ahaziah, King of Israel, and Elijah (II Kings 1:1 ff.). It seems that good King Ahaziah was not so very good. He ruled in the manner of his father, Ahab, worshiped Baal, and did what was evil in the sight of the Lord. He tripped one day and fell through the lattice in his upper chamber, and being anxious about his condition, he sent messengers to "go, inquire of Baalzebub, the god of Ekron, whether I shall recover from this sickness." The messengers were intercepted by Elijah, God's emissary in Israel.

The first thing Elijah asked the messengers was, "Is it because there is no God in Israel that you are sending to inquire of Baalzebub, the god of Ekron?" Then he prophesied that Ahaziah would die. Later, when the king was told that the man who met the messengers wore a garment of haircloth, with a girdle of leather about his loins, he promptly guessed, and correctly, "It is Elijah the Tishbite."

Ahaziah in great anger sent a captain with a group of fifty soldiers to call Elijah down from the hill where he was staying. Elijah refused, saying, "If I am a man of God, let fire come down from heaven and consume you and your fifty." And they were consumed. The king sent another captain with fifty, and there was a repetition of the event. The next captain was a more cautious soul and, kneeling before Elijah, entreated him to save them all and come down from the hill. Elijah complied and went to the king, asking, "Thus says the LORD, 'Because you have sent messengers to inquire of Baalzebub, the god of Ekron, —is it because there is no God in Israel to inquire of his word?—therefore you shall not come down from the bed to which you have gone, but you shall surely die.' "

The scribes who accused Jesus of being possessed by Beelzebul had come down from Jerusalem, Mark's testimony to Jesus' increasing fame. They came apparently to make damning accusations about Jesus to his followers, and they claimed that Jesus cast out demons by the prince of demons. There is no tradition in Rabbinic sources, or in apochrypha or pseudepigrapha that Beelzebul(b) was considered the prince of demons.[24] Nor is there anywhere in Jewish literature a reference to Satan being called "Beelzebul." The change of spelling (bub to bul) is perplexing, and there seem to be three possibilities: (1) the name has been changed to "Beelzebul," i.e., "lord of the flies," as a satiric corruption of the name of the god of Ekron for the purpose of insult; (2) the name has been derived from a Hebrew word, and the suffix, "zebul," i.e., "height," "abode," "dwelling," would suggest the meaning of "lord of the dwelling," referring either to the air or to the possessed in whom he dwells; (3) the word is connected with an Aramaic word of similar sound which means "enemy."[25] The last possibility more nearly fits the Marcan passage. For example, the scribes were unable to recognize the presence of the power of God in their land and accused Jesus of being in the hire of the enemy, Satan. Since they were from Jerusalem, their action indicates that he was singled out as the enemy by the power group there, which he particularly threatened. Mark's Jesus had already, by his actions and his teaching, indicated that he believed the worship and leadership of the scribes to be corrupt and alien to God's will. The scribes had come from the Temple (the king's dwelling?) and reproached Jesus for being the enemy, in the employ of Satan; yet was it not obvious that Jesus was pitted against Satan, since Satan would scarcely rise against himself, and Jesus had been casting out demons, satanic powers? As for the question of whether there was a God in Israel, the answer would appear to be yes. The scribes were warned not to cause the division of the house (of Israel), for a house divided could not stand. Further, Jesus indirectly warned that he intended to plunder a remnant from Israel, i.e., when he spoke of plundering the strong man's goods after he has been bound, implying that he would overcome the ruling powers since they had fallen into league with Satan.

The contempt of the scribes for the spirit Jesus possessed, i.e., the Holy Spirit given him at baptism, prompted Jesus to warn them against blasphemy. Those who blaspheme against the Holy Spirit never have forgiveness, but are guilty of an eternal sin. Eternity is a long time—those two companies who came out from Ahaziah to Elijah were promptly dispatched to it by the fire from heaven. Mark believed it was the prevailing rulers of the house of Israel who were possessed by demons and unclean spirits; they did not know where to go in Israel to inquire the word of God.

Who Is My Family?

During the preceding discussion, Jesus' mother and brothers came and waited outside for him. His friends had already come to seize him because they thought him beside himself. When told his family was outside asking for him, he declared that his true family were those who do the will of God and to these he gave allegiance ahead of his blood kin. When Moses had come down from Mt. Sinai with the tablets and discovered that Aaron had in his absence fashioned a golden calf for the people to worship, he cried: "Who is on the LORD's side? Come to me" (Ex. 32:26). The Levites aligned themselves with Moses and were ordered by him to slay brothers, companions, and neighbors. When they did as they were commanded, Moses told them, "Today you have ordained yourselves for the service of the LORD, each one at the cost of his son and of his brother, that he may bestow a blessing upon you this day" (v. 29). As it was necessary in the first exodus for the Levites, the religious leaders of Israel, to choose between God and family, so it was likewise necessary in the new exodus, and Jesus Christ, the replacement for Levi, must choose between family and service to God. "Who is on the LORD's side? Come to me," becomes in Mark, "Whoever does the will of God is my brother, and sister, and mother" (Mark 3:35).

The Parables

Again Jesus began to teach beside the sea. The "sea" is mentioned no less than eighteen times in Mark. The first three times that he withdrew to the sea he did so immediately after an altercation with the scribes. The first and third times he taught, the second time he healed. In almost every instance, Mark pictures the light of the truth and power of God in the spirit of Jesus against the background of the sea, the symbol of darkness, chaos, and death.

In this instance, Jesus literally sat on the face of the deep, since he was forced to separate himself from the crowd of people gathered by sitting in a boat offshore. For the first time he taught in parables, and he began with the parables of the sower. These describe Jesus' method of spreading the word of God's delivering love and the results that might be expected when the word fell on different ears. This is not so much a prediction of the outcome of Jesus' ministry as it is an apologia for what actually had happened. It had already begun to unfold in this manner. The disciples were taught in more depth than the crowds, and Jesus paraphrased Isa. 6:9 f., when he said the crowds were taught in parables "so that they may indeed see but not perceive, and may indeed hear but not understand; lest they should turn again, and be forgiven" (Mark 4:12). Remember, all prophecy must be fulfilled, and even that which had been fulfilled in the Old Testament was not eliminated, for God's word, once spoken, endured forever. It was Isaiah's task to preach to a faithless nation in such a way that she would not understand or perceive until God's will had been accomplished, and it is to be likewise for Jesus.

A lamp, Jesus stated, was not meant to be hidden. The light of understanding had been sent to Israel by God, not to hide his word, but to illumine it. What God has hidden previously, he would now reveal to those who listen and look carefully. The disciples were warned that he who heard the word and accepted it wholeheartedly would receive increased understanding, but he who would not would have what understanding he had of God's word taken away.

The closing two parables of this section speak of the mystery of the growth of the Kingdom of God and what great results can be expected from such small beginnings. The parable of the mustard seed parallels Ezek. 17:22 ff., in which God declared he would grow a lofty cedar from a small tender branch to shade the world and shelter the animals. This was perhaps considered a messianic prophecy because of the use of the word "branch."

Rebuking the Wind and the Sea

There follows in the Gospel the first of many crossings of the sea. Apparently several boats went. Even though Mark says they left the crowd, he obviously intended to convey the idea that a number of people accompanied them. They encountered a storm so severe that the boat began to fill. Jesus was sleeping when they awakened him with a cry that sounds as if it had come straight out of the wilderness of the exodus, when the Israelites, in great fear, claimed that Moses had brought them out of Egypt to die (Ex. 14:10 f.). "Teacher, do you not care if we perish?" (Mark 4:38.) When Jesus awoke he rebuked the sea with, "Peace! Be still!" Here Jesus addressed the sea as if it had a malevolent spirit, using the same admonition he had spoken to the unclean spirit (ch. 1:25). The wind ceased and the sea became calm. Jesus chided the disciples for their lack of faith, even as Moses had told the Israelites to "fear not, stand firm, and see the salvation of the LORD" (Ex. 14:13). Jesus had just previously warned the disciples with the parables of the sower how they must heed his words and believe. The disciples' awe at his power over the elements prompted the question, "Who then is this, that even wind and sea obey him?" Only the power of God is efficacious to control the wind and the sea, and Mark's story surely implies an answer to the question, i.e., that Jesus was the Son of God.

Legion

Following the crossing of the sea there is a curious account concerning a demoniac. They had come into pagan country, and when they left the boat they encountered a man possessed by an unclean spirit who lived among the tombs. Although he was not dead, he lived among the dead in a land that had no understanding of God's word. He was often put into fetters and chains to keep him in bondage. Night and day he cried out and in his anguish often injured himself. In view of the interpretation of the previous healing incidents, it should not be difficult to understand Mark's symbolism. Israel herself had been in bondage in a pagan land, and she was still in bondage, held in the chains and fetters of the law by her religious leaders; Jesus had come to set the captives free. She was living among the dead, for old Israel was the same as dead when she lost her firstborn, Levi.

The man ran to Jesus, and it is unclear whether Mark intends to convey that it was he or the unclean spirit who addressed Jesus as "Son of the Most High God." In view of the fact that this is the first individual involved in a healing narrative who is told: "Go home to your friends, and tell them how much the Lord has done for you, and how he has had mercy on you," it may be Mark's intention that his reader understand it was the man who so addressed Jesus.

Jesus commanded the unclean spirit to come out of the man, as he would have desired to remove the unclean spirit from Israel. When Jesus asked the spirit its name, he was told, "Legion." There is no other instance where the name of a spirit comes into consideration, which alone makes this incident remarkable. Legion begged not to be sent from the country, which is perhaps an interesting twist on the exodus story if one recalls that Pharaoh, toward the end of his conflict with Moses, told the Israelites they could go to worship their God, but not too far. Legion requested and received permission to enter a large herd of swine nearby, which promptly rushed into the sea and were drowned, even as the legions of Egypt who had kept Israel chained in bondage had drowned in the sea.

This is the only instance in Mark of multiple unclean spirits. The first four healing narratives were concerned with the sickness of the spirit of Israel, God's chosen. The fifth healing was a warning to those who would stretch out a hand against the man from God. The hand would be restored, but the defiled altar at which they worshiped would fall. It was clearly a warning to the scribes, and the incident was quickly followed by the official naming of the disciples. Levi's name did not appear among those chosen for a reconstituted Israel.

The scribes were warned that if a strong man was bound, his house could be plundered. Legion was bound in a herd of swine and drowned in the sea, and the man whom they had held captive, often in fetters and chains, in a state of living death, was found sitting, clothed and in his right mind. In symbol, does this not mean that Levi and the bondage to the law had been eliminated from the new Israel, and that she was now free and in her right mind to be God's covenanted people? The people who came to witness what had happened, in their fear, begged Jesus to depart from the neighborhood, even as the Egyptians had urgently pleaded with Moses and the Israelites to leave Egypt after the death of all the firstborn of Egypt. Now, symbolically through Jesus in the new exodus, the death of the firstborn of the captors of Israel had been accomplished, and Jesus and the disciples were urgently requested to leave. There is something ironically amusing about Legion being allowed to enter a herd of swine and thereby be destroyed, considering that the Jews believed swine to be unclean animals and that the Jews were forbidden to eat pork.

Summary

Much of the symbolism in this passage suggests the exodus in the Old Testament. Jesus is revealed as one who had power over the wind and the water. Upon arrival in a pagan country, he found a man who was in bondage to Legion, and when Legion was destroyed the man was free. Jesus and the disciples were begged by the inhabitants to depart from the neighborhood. Israel of old had been in bondage in a pagan land. When Moses, representing God, had come to seek her release, his final warning was that the firstborn of the nation would be destroyed if Israel were not set free. When Egypt still demurred, God's threat was carried out, and Israel was begged by the Egyptians to leave the country.

This is the first healing incident in which Jesus instructed the person healed to go home to his friends and tell about God's delivering love and mercy. The man began to proclaim the word in the region of the Decapolis, which was Gentile and pagan. With the "death" of Legion, i.e., Levi, God's chosen people, now in their right mind, could indeed be the people covenanted to God and become a blessing to the nations—the word could now be carried to the Gentiles.

Chapter 5

CAN NEW ISRAEL KEEP
THE COVENANT?

Mark 5:21 to 6:29

Jairus

WHEN JESUS ARRIVED across the sea a great crowd
gathered around him. One of the rulers of the synagogue
came pleading for his help. His name was Jairus, a name
possibly derived from the Hebrew meaning "he will
arouse."[26] It is probable that Mark did intend some special
symbolism by the name. This is suggested if for no other
reason than that he used the proper name of only one
other person (outside the disciples), i.e., Bartimaeus
(ch. 10:46). Jairus' supplication was for Jesus to "lay
hands" on his daughter, who was at the point of death,
that she might be *saved* (not "made well" as in the RSV)
and *live*. When Jesus made no answer to the man, the
reader is left to wonder whether Jesus went with Jairus,
or Jairus followed Jesus. There is implicit in Jesus' lack
of reply the same kind of "refusing to pay any attention"
that is described in v. 36. Jesus apparently was not dis-
tressed by the report or the supplication, but continued
on his way, and it seems likely that Mark intended for the
reader to understand that Jairus followed Jesus.

The Woman with a Flow of Blood

Among the crowd who followed Jesus was a woman
who suffered from a "flow of blood." Mark says she had

suffered *twelve* years. Surely the deliberate use of the number of years was scarcely an accident. Is it not possible that after ridding Israel of Legion/Levi, the new Israel, composed of the twelve disciples thus far, is the patient with whom we are confronted? This is a case of ritual impurity, but it is not one caused by demon possession or an unclean spirit. It was not something that had entered the woman from the outside which caused her affliction; it was something inherently wrong within herself which rendered her unclean, i.e., which caused her to be in a state of sin, suffering from a broken relationship to God. There are no further healing narratives in Mark dealing with demon possession, for the healing henceforth is not for a sick Israel in bondage to the law, but for a weak, struggling, new Israel, not completely free within herself for the right understanding of her role as God's covenanted people. She must learn what it means to walk in the covenant.

Mark says the woman had suffered under many physicians, spending all she had but nevertheless growing worse. The criticism of her physicians was probably, in Mark's symbolism, a criticism of the Pharisees, who practiced medicine in the field of ritual impurity.[27] The spirit of the Pharisees had robbed Israel of her relationship to God, rendering her unclean, and her condition had worsened through the years until nothing could save her short of a new exodus.

The woman, who had heard reports about Jesus, came up behind him in the crowd to touch his garment, believing she would be healed. Immediately it was so, and at the same time Jesus perceived that the "power proceeding from him went forth." The Greek word for power is the same one that Mark uses in speaking of the power with which the Kingdom of God comes (ch. 9:1); in speaking of the Parousia (return in power and glory) of the Son of Man (ch. 13:26); and in referring to the power of

God (chs. 12:24; 14:62). It was this power, which Mark says Jesus possessed, which could cleanse the spirit of an Israel who in her right mind had accepted the call to become God's chosen people. As yet, the new Israel had not rightly or fully understood the meaning of accepting the call to covenant, but she has shown by following Jesus that she believed it was his power that would heal her and give her right understanding. This power, not available without belief, had now, symbolically through the woman's believing touch, been infused into Israel itself.

The disciples remonstrated with Jesus when he turned and asked who had touched him, but the woman, realizing "what had been done to her" (Mark does not say, "knowing that she had been made well" or "healed"), fell down before him, and told him the whole truth. Israel has begun to receive the power that Jesus had in his possession to bestow. Jesus said, "Daughter, your faith has made you well; go in peace, and be healed of your disease." (Ch. 5:34.) The last phrase might better be translated "be restored from your sinful condition," for the word translated as "disease" means "scourge" or "afflictions of the sinner," as well as "bodily illness."[28]

The fact that the woman's touching Jesus would have rendered him ceremonially unclean was completely ignored. And unlike the cleansing of the leper, no mention is made of the necessity of going to the priest for the ritual cleansing demanded by the law. The demand of the ritual law is no longer valid.

The Child Is Dead

All this time, presumably, Jairus still accompanied Jesus, although Jesus had not turned attention to him. Mark seems to convey the idea that Jesus could not do anything about Jairus' daughter until after the episode with the woman had occurred, i.e., until his power had been transmitted to Israel. As long as new Israel still retained some of the old sickness and uncleanness, a residual from her captivity under the old leaders, she would not have the power to serve. While Jesus was yet speaking to the woman, someone came from the ruler's house with the news that the child was dead and there was, therefore, no reason to bother Jesus further. He ignored the word that was brought, and addressed himself rather to the father, a ruler of the synagogue, who has been informed that his child is dead. He said, "Do not fear, only believe." (Ch. 5:36.) Even as belief had restored the woman from her uncleanness, belief in Jesus' spirit was the necessary ingredient for the restoration of Jairus' child who had been declared dead.

From this point Mark's Jesus devoted his full attention to the situation, and taking with him only those disciples who had obviously grown closest to him—Peter, James, and John—he went home with Jairus. When they arrived they were confronted with a tumult, and people weeping and wailing loudly. This phraseology is peculiar to Mark. Is he suggesting symbolically that the word had spread that Levi, firstborn of the ruler of the synagogue, i.e., congregation of Israel, was dead, and as a result Israel no longer existed? This is a mourning scene, although it seems scarcely likely there would have been time to have obtained professional mourners for the child since, after all, Jairus had just heard of the death of the child himself. When Jesus entered upon the scene he asked why the people were weeping, since the child was not dead, only sleeping. Even though Israel appeared dead, having lost her firstborn, Jesus says rather, "No, the young child, the new Israel, is not dead, but has just not yet awakened to the task before her." The word Mark uses for "sleeping" is one that can be interpreted as the "sleep of death," as well as "death," but Mark's Jesus had specifically denied death. It is possible that the word could be understood to denote a comatose condition, which would be a fitting description of the infant Israel, which as yet was unconscious of the task before her. The Greek word that Mark uses for "child" is an affectionate diminutive which was used for children of all ages.

The people laughed derisively at Jesus. The expression Mark uses contains an unusually bold verb not found elsewhere in the New Testament, and can be translated as "to deride" or "jeer at." The contrast between the simple, appealing faith of Jairus when he first went to Jesus, that of the woman in the crowd, and that of the jeering people is notable. Although the crowd is not identified, Mark's implication is that they had little faith that Jesus could raise up the child/Israel from what appeared to all as death. Jesus forcibly put them all out and went in to the child, taking only the father, the mother, and the three disciples. When Mark reveals that Jairus was a ruler of the synagogue and the father of the child, he may be suggesting that although Israel had traditionally had her life in the synagogues, as long as that continues to be true, the new child, Israel, would remain in the tradition of the synagogue and would be as one dead. Only when she had the spirit and understanding of Jesus would she be able to rise.

The Child Arises

When Jesus and those with him came to where the child lay, Jesus took her by the hand and, calling her by an affectionate name, said, "Talitha, cum," which means, "Little lamb, I say to you arise." "Talitha, cum" is a transliteration of an Aramaic phrase; "talitha" is the feminine for "lamb" or "youth," but the verb "cum" is masculine. While the RSV has the feminine form "cumi" (as does the ASV), there seems to be little doubt that the original was the masculine form.[29] There is only one instance where Mark does not translate the Aramaic into Greek for his Gentile readers (ch. 11:9 f.). While the phrase "talitha, cum" is translated, the original Aramaic has a subtly different connotation because of the mixed genders of noun and verb. The Greek verb in this instance would have no gender. The reason for using the masculine form of the verb, even though Jesus was presumably speaking to a girl, must surely mean that Mark was in fact referring to the new Israel, here represented by Peter, James, and John.

The Greek word translated as "Arise!" is the imperative form of the verb. It might equally well be translated "Wake up!" So again Mark has used a word with a double meaning, and it shouldn't be difficult to understand why Jesus would say to Israel either "Arise" or "Wake up." It should be remembered also that Jairus' name could mean "he awakens" or "he will arouse," so that everything in the passage points to an awakening. The figure "twelve" is again deliberately inserted, which Mark says is the age of the child, and having established by his word game that Jesus from this time forth will be working with a new Israel, the Twelve, Mark does not again insert such a sly hint into the remaining healing narratives.

Immediately, the child got up and walked. There is a forcefulness inherent in the Greek word translated in the RSV as "got up" (elsewhere, "arose") and this is reinforced by "immediately." The tenses of the two verbs "arose" and "walked" are carefully distinguished,[30] and the phrase would accurately be rendered into English as, "arose and *continued* walking."

They Were Amazed

The jeers of the unbelieving crowd give way to the amazement of the witnesses present in the room. Even they, evidently, had not expected Jesus to accomplish a miracle quite so unbelievable. Their amazement was *strongly expressed,* indicating that something utterly unexpected had occurred. The text states that Jesus "strictly charged that no one should know *this*" (italics ours). Previous injunctions to silence have been couched in terms forbidding anyone to "speak" of what they have witnessed. Here Mark says they are not to let anyone *know this;* i.e., none is to know that even the three most intimate disciples, the same who were to be with him at the transfiguration and later in Gethsemane, did not believe that Christ could call a tiny remnant into being a new Israel, heal her of her wrong understanding, infuse her with new life, and cause her to *walk* and *continue walking.* "Which is easier, to say . . . [to Israel], 'Your sins are forgiven,' or to say, 'Rise, take up your pallet and walk'?" (Ch. 2:9.) It would make little sense to interpret Jesus' command to silence as referring to the raising of the child if only because of the crowd of "mourners" gathered outside the house who believed her dead. Such an injunction could scarcely be taken seriously.

Jesus ordered the raised one to be fed. His order was not, seemingly, directed at anyone; it more nearly suggests a promised feeding and would fit Mark's exodus pattern: Israel is called, delivered, i.e., saved (which is what Jairus had asked of Jesus), and fed.

The New Character of Jesus

Perhaps the one most interesting feature about these last three healings, the demoniac, the woman with a flow of blood, and Jairus' daughter, is the visible change in the character of Jesus himself. He is, in these narratives, an entirely different person from that stern, angry, sarcastic healer of the first portion of the Gospel. He is here tender, kind, and solicitous, seeking to nurse and nourish these afflicted ones. The early picture of him as someone impersonal has completely vanished. With the deliverance of the new Israel from captivity under Levi, symbolized by the exorcism of Legion, Jesus' healing is no longer directed to old Israel, but to the new Israel, his followers.

The latter two healings, the woman with a flow of blood and Jairus' daughter, together with the next healing narrative, the Syrophoenician woman's daughter, are all concerned with women. As symbolic figures for the new Israel, it would appear most fitting that those symbols are feminine in character. Christ was the "head of the church," and the church was to be subject to him as wives to husbands, an understanding that is a prominent metaphor in the epistle to the Ephesians (Eph., ch. 5). Jesus had earlier referred to himself as the bridegroom to his followers (Mark 2:19 f.).

Rejection at Home

Jesus made his way with his disciples back to his own country. At the beginning of ch. 6, Mark narrates the last sorrowful leave-taking from traditional Israel. On the Sabbath, Jesus began to teach in the synagogue. He was apparently regarded by those present as something of an upstart. They questioned his humble origins, and were astonished that one from such a background should have his wisdom and power, the source of which they did not understand. They were offended by him, and Jesus declared finally the inability of his prophecy to be heard and accepted by the house of Israel. His ministry from this time forth was a changed one. Mark brings him back into Galilee proper on only brief occasions (chs. 6:53 ff.; 8:11 ff.), and other times he and the disciples merely pass through. Nor do we find him anymore teaching and preaching in the synagogues in the Gospel. With the exception of the cleansing of and teaching in the Temple in Jersualem during the last week, Mark does not again tell that Jesus entered a synagogue. From this time forth, his ministry was concerned only with those who would see and hear him gladly and would, because of their belief in him and his mission, indeed perceive and understand. The lack of belief among his own people precluded any mighty deliverance. Mark relates the healing, in one instance, of only a few who understood and believed. The hearts of those remaining were hardened against him to such an extent that Jesus himself is pictured by Mark as amazed.

Sending Out the Disciples

Having abandoned hope for old Israel, which had proved itself dead to him and to the new exodus, Jesus turned away from his affiliation with his own people and turned his attention to the new Israel and the task before her. Could she walk? and continue walking? Could she proclaim the necessity of repentance and the promise of deliverance to the world? To prove that she was undeniably capable of keeping the covenant, the disciples were called by Jesus, instilled with his power, and sent to preach that men should repent. They were to cast out the unclean spirit from among those separated from God who would hear and accept.

The Death of John

After the disciples had been dispatched, Mark writes, "King Herod heard of it; for Jesus' name had become known" (ch. 6:14), but Mark does not inform his readers exactly what it was that King Herod heard. There is the implication, however, since this passage follows the one concerning the healing, the resuscitation, and the mission of new Israel, that this is what Herod heard.

There are historical inaccuracies in Mark's story of the death of John, e.g., Herod was not a king, merely a regional ruler, but these do not detract from its place in the Gospel. Herod and his marital and political complications are not Mark's primary concern. The parallel to the relationship between Elijah and Ahab and Jezebel is evident. Jesus, like Elisha, who had "come after" Elijah, is presented as one who inherited a "double portion" of

John's spirit, and in time Jesus' disciples far overshadowed those of John.

There is also a strong parallel to the death of Jesus himself in this account of the death of John. Pilate plays an uncomfortable Herod in the condemnation, and both Jesus and John were victims of treacherous betrayal.

Summary

In the passage concerning the Gerasene demoniac, Mark, with the symbolism of the casting out of Legion, inferred the demise of old Israel. Historic Israel had not kept God's covenant, had not been willing to walk—and continue walking—the roads and byroads of the world to carry the message of God's loving care to the world. A new Israel was called into being, with Jesus, who was infused with the power of God, at her head. The tyranny of the Levitical priesthood, which kept the people in servitude to the law, was eliminated.

The new Israel, small, insignificant, woefully lacking in faith and understanding, not yet perceiving her task under the covenant, must be carefully nurtured and nourished with the right understanding, cleansed of all vestiges of the old taint, and infused with the power of God, present in Jesus Christ. She must be raised to her feet to walk and continue walking. There existed scornful lack of faith in Jesus' ability to accomplish that which history seemed to call impossible. Jesus, nevertheless, called a remnant of twelve to its feet, and sent the disciples out two by two to carry the good news. Israel had been called, delivered from captivity, and now must be brought to a full understanding of what was meant by her covenant relationship to God.

Chapter 6

THE EXTENSION OF THE KINGDOM TO THE GENTILES

Mark 6:30 to 9:1

MARK HAS DRAMATIZED symbolically the calling of the remnant out of its spiritual captivity into a fulfillment of the covenant relationship with God. Because the covenant had been so much misunderstood, Mark now shows, through the feeding narratives, Jesus delineating the meaning of the covenant and its implications for the Israelite remnant, who are presented as still unaware of its full meaning. As has already been indicated, Jesus is depicted by Mark as understanding that God's loving care was intended for all men, and that Israel was called to be God's servant and messenger to call all men to God. The inclusiveness of the covenant relationship is to be symbolized in the feeding narratives, and as will be seen, Mark developed a truly ingenious numerological symbolism to make his point.

When the disciples returned from their mission, Jesus invited them to retreat for quiet reflection, but they could not escape from the people. Jesus, as ever compassionate, began to teach them and kept them until late in the day. This is Mark's setting for the first feeding narrative. (Ch. 6:35 ff.)

There are strong undercurrents of the Old Testament in the feeding narratives. The first bears a strong resemblance to II Kings 4:42 ff., where Elisha fed a company of one hundred men with the firstfruits of harvest which were brought to him, and there was not only a sufficient amount from a small provision, there was some left over. And as there were two feeding narratives in the wilderness under Moses (Ex., ch. 16, and Num., ch. 11), so there are two feeding narratives in Mark. The second story of the feedings in the Old Testament was one involving a mixed multitude, and the second in Mark, as will be discussed, was probably intended to mean a mixed multitude, including Gentiles.

Symbolism of the Elements

Not much is usually made of the presence of fish in these stories, but it is present at both feedings and is often regarded as the symbolic representation of the quail of the Old Testament, which Israel received along with the manna (Ex. 16:13). Fish was often a substitute in Western Christianity for the wine in the pictorial portrayal of the Last Supper. The fish was the Jewish symbol for the Messiah and became the Christian symbol for the Christ. It was a sacramental food and eating it represented a sacramental communion with God. Paul called the Rock that followed Israel in the exodus "Christ" (I Cor. 10:4), and from a sacramental point of view, to eat fish "was a way of taking into oneself the fluid which embodied the life or being of the Savior,"[31] so the fluid (blood) of Christ's body at the Last Supper was a substitute for the fish at the feedings. While Paul and the Synoptics trace the Eucharist to the bread and the wine of the Last Supper, John traces it to the miracle of the fishes and loaves, and recounts a postresurrection bread-fish feeding. Bread in baskets, together with fish, became a symbol representing the Eucharist.[32]

One of the earliest ideas encountered in early Christian art is the association of a basket of bread with the Eucharist. There are numerous pictures of Christ multiplying the loaves (usually seven) with a rod such as Moses used. Baskets were profoundly symbolic in Christianity and were perhaps derived from Jewish prototypes. In art, they ordinarily suggested a ceremonial use of bread and wine in Judaism and in Christianity. In Jewish tradition, it appears that the baskets made their appearance only in connection with the Festival of Firstfruits, a festival connected with spiritual salvation and immortality. Firstfruits are very significant in the New Testament. Christ was called the firstfruits of those risen from the dead.[33]

The First Feeding Narrative

There are a number of reasons for believing that Mark intended the first feeding to be regarded as a "Jewish" feeding and the second one to be regarded as a "Gentile" feeding. The religious treatment of the food itself is significant. In every orthodox meal, the head of the family comes to the table with freshly washed hands, and, blessing the bread, breaks it. Jesus blessed the bread in the first feeding, which would be a natural thing to do at a Jewish meal, but at the second feeding, Mark says that he gave thanks for the bread, thus eliminating the traditional blessing which would probably have been without meaning to a Gentile audience. Additionally, the geographic location suggests a difference, as the first incident appears to take place in Jewish territory, and the second in Gentile country.[34]

In both feeding narratives the disciples expressed dismay at the lack of food and disbelief that so many could be fed, especially in remote country. In the first story, Jesus told the disciples themselves to feed the crowd, but as they had not yet understood the kind of food of which he spoke, they answered him with sarcasm. The need and the disciples' response echo Ps. 78, which recounts the exodus:

They tested God in their heart
  by demanding the food they craved.
They spoke against God, saying,
  "Can God spread a table in the wilderness?
He smote the rock so that water gushed out
  and streams overflowed.
Can he also give bread,
  or provide meat for his people?"

(Vs. 18 ff.)

And they ate and were well filled,
  for he gave them what they craved.

(V. 29.)

Much has been made of the numerical symbolism of
the loaves and baskets in Mark. (See Farrer, Bowman, etc.)
Certainly the numbers of the people and the loaves and
the baskets were no accident of history. The five loaves to
feed the five thousand find their significance in the story
of David and the showbread (I Sam. 21:1 ff.). David
was fleeing from Solomon and had with him a group of
followers. He asked the priest for something to eat, and
as there was nothing there but the twelve loaves of the
bread of the presence, which were placed daily on the
altar to remind Israel that the bread of life came from
the hand of God, David asked for five of the loaves. Mark
obviously adopted the symbolism of twelve loaves to use
in his feeding narratives to symbolize that all bread comes
from the hand of God—we are indebted to God for the
sustenance of life. Mark's Jesus is the liaison of God's
word between God and man, and as will be shown, the
feedings also symbolize the nurturing of a proper understanding of the covenant with God in addition to the
understanding that God is the sustainer of life.

As five loaves were sufficient to feed David and his followers, so five now symbolize sufficiency to feed Jesus and
his followers. After the multitude had been fed, there

remained twelve small baskets, enough for the continued feeding of Israel, the twelve. Symbolically, seven loaves of the twelve loaves of showbread remained.

Walking on the Water

Following the first feeding narrative, Mark relates a curious story, fraught with the symbolism of the sea, the wind, and Jesus' role. He says that the disciples had gotten into the boat and left Jesus on the shore. They ran into heavy winds, and Jesus came walking on the water to them. Even though they were in evident distress, Mark says that Jesus meant to pass them by, but when they saw him, thinking he was some sort of apparition on the water, they cried out in fear. Their cry touched him, and he got into the boat with them and the wind became calm. The disciples were amazed, and Mark tells us their amazement was due to the fact that they had not understood about the loaves because their hearts were hardened.

Obviously, there is intended more by this story than a mere demonstration of some miraculous power residing in Jesus. It is probably a reflection of the prophecy of Isaiah about the exile of Israel of old. The Twelve, like Israel of old, had been called to a new exodus to be the servants of God. They were called in the covenant to be given as servants to the people, a light to the nations, to open eyes that were blind, to bring prisoners from the dungeon of captivity (Isa. 42:6 f.). Israel had been called and delivered from the bondage of her captors, led into the wilderness and fed, but subsequently failed to understand her role as servant and was sent into exile. The new Twelve had been called to fulfill the covenant, delivered from the bondage of their captors, and, when taken to a lonely place where they worried about food, were fed in a manner presented as no less miraculous than was God's gift of manna and quail. Yet they had not understood, and in Mark's imagery, he implies that Jesus meant to exile them by passing them by. They suffered from the same infirmities as Israel of old, about whom Isaiah wrote:

> Hear, you deaf;
>   and look, you blind, that you may see!
> Who is blind but my servant,
>   or deaf as my messenger whom I send?
> Who is blind as my dedicated one,
>   or blind as the servant of the LORD?
> He sees many things, but does not observe them;
>   his ears are open, but he does not hear.
>
>   (Isa. 42:18 ff.)

Because Israel had refused her role as God's servant, God had banished her into Babylonian exile. But even as God had repented of the exile in the Old Testament and returned a remnant, so Jesus repented and went to the disciples when they cried out to him in their anguish.

> But now thus says the LORD,
>   he who created you, O Jacob,
>   he who formed you, O Israel:
> "Fear not, for I have redeemed you;
>   I have called you by name, you are mine.
> When you pass through the waters I will be with you;
>   and through the rivers, they shall not overwhelm you."
>
>   (Isa. 43:1 f.)

When the wind calmed and they had crossed the sea, they were besieged by people who crowded around Jesus with their sick. Even those who touched the fringe of his garment, we are told, were made well.

The Letter Versus the Spirit of the Law

There were Pharisees and scribes from Jerusalem who, Mark says, also came to Jesus. They did not ask for healing; they complained that he and the disciples ate with unwashed hands. The Pharisees purified not only themselves after being in the marketplace among the people, and before eating. They also kept many other traditions of the elders; e.g., they purified all cooking and eating vessels. When they asked Jesus why the disciples did not keep tradition, his answer was from Isaiah (ch. 29:13):

> This people honors me with their lips,
> but their heart is far from me;
> in vain do they worship me,
> teaching as doctrines the precepts of men.
> (Mark 7:6 f.)

Jesus accused them of idolatry of tradition, preferring the letter of man's law to the spirit of God's commandments. Tradition excused them from an open, honest, and loving relationship to men, including their own parents, whom they had been commanded to honor, for they could and did use a pledge to the Temple to exonerate themselves from caring for their parents.

Jesus then launched into a lecture on the nature of defilement. It is not that which enters a man or clings to him from the outside which results in defilement; it is, rather, the inner corruption of man's hardened and unrepenting heart which is the true defilement. It should never be forgotten through what profound questioning and personal anxiety these ideas concerning unclean food, etc., were finally grasped by the Christian community. The Torah is explicit about unclean food: even a "clean" animal was rendered impure if it was not slain in a certain manner.

Thus Jesus challenged both the written and the oral law, and while Mark does not actually mention food, but merely the manner of eating, the impression is that food itself, i.e., in the sense of that which becomes part of a man from that which is outside him, was Jesus' concern. The implications, however, were vastly broader. Jesus had already, in defiance of the law, touched a leper and appeared unconcerned at the touch of a woman who was ceremonially unclean. It was not these external elements, even any element taken internally, which were defiling; it was, rather, one's attitude toward God and fellowman. A person is defiled if his attitude sacrifices God's moral commandment to tradition or ritual law, or if his lack of regard and respect for his neighbor discloses a self given to evil thoughts, fornication, theft, murder, adultery, coveting, etc. (Mark 7:21).

The Syrophoenician Woman's Daughter

Following Jesus' encounter with the Pharisees, once again he and the disciples made their way to the Gentile country around Tyre and Sidon. An attempt to remain in obscurity failed, and Mark says he was accosted by a Greek woman whose daughter had an unclean spirit. To the Pharisees it would have been a redundance to say that a Gentile had an unclean spirit; to be Gentile was to be unclean. Upon answering her supplication, Jesus said merely that the children should be fed first, and their food should not be usurped for the "dogs" (a common word used in connection with Gentiles). The woman replied that the dogs were at least allowed the crumbs under the table, even if they weren't allowed to partake of food at the table itself. Jesus, pleased by the woman's remark, told her that her request had been granted. When she returned home she found the demon had left her child. Not only has Mark's Jesus declared to the Pharisees that nothing— food, vessels, the marketplace—outside a man could defile him, but with the symbolism of this healing narrative (the one Gentile healing of the total thirteen healing narratives), Jesus is depicted as declaring that Gentiles could no longer be considered to be possessed by an unclean spirit, but were invited to partake of the same food as Israel. They were accepted and healed by God.

The Deaf Man with an Impediment

Israel, the twelve disciples, was being prepared to hear and understand the true meaning of her relationship to God, but she yet suffered from lack of perception and inability to be messengers of God's word. Of these infirmities she must be healed. To symbolize Israel's further healing and preparation to become God's servant to the world, Mark relates Jesus' encounter with a man who was deaf and suffered from a speech impediment. Israel must have her ears opened to God's authentic word, and she must learn to speak that word correctly (for that is what the Greek verb, here translated as "spoke plainly," means), and not simply honor it with her lips while living in allegiance to man's tradition and law. Mark likely had in the back of his mind the passages in Isaiah concerning hearing and seeing (Isa. 29:18 ff.; 35:5 f.).

The reaction of those present to the cure of the man was one of complete amazement, more strongly expressed here than anywhere else in the Gospel. They marveled that Jesus could make the deaf and dumb to hear and speak. Mark has already made abundantly clear that such amazement was certainly not without foundation. When, indeed, had Israel really heard God's word and understood, and when had she spoken it plainly for all to hear? Who, indeed, was as blind, deaf, and dumb as God's messenger? In order to make more powerful the image of the transfer of Jesus' personal spirit to Israel, Mark says that Jesus literally put his fingers in the man's ears and spat, touching his tongue.

The Second Feeding Narrative

Now that the Gentiles had been accepted to receive God's food/word, and Israel had been given her hearing and a tongue to speak God's word, Mark relates the story

of the second feeding, which took place in Gentile country, and symbolically is the first feeding of the Gentiles
with God's food/word. A great crowd of about four thousand people had gathered around Jesus, and had been with
him three days while he taught them. These "three" days
may be intended by Mark to parallel the three days God
told Moses to consecrate the people, at which time he
would appear to them in a cloud so that the people could
hear him speak and believe in him forever (Ex. 19:
10 ff.).

Mark 13:27 states that the coming of the Son of Man
in power would be followed by his sending out messengers
to gather the elect from the four winds, and from the ends
of the earth to the ends of heaven. The four thousand are
those of God's children gathered from the four corners of
the earth to receive his blessing. As Gentiles, they would
symbolically be from the seventy nations of the Gentiles.
Seven loaves would be an appropriate amount to feed
them, and there were seven loaves at hand, remaining,
symbolically, from the twelve loaves of God's presence,
five having been used in the first feeding. There is another precedent for the use of the number "seven" in
connection with Gentiles. In the early church, after Gentiles had become a fair portion of those who followed the
Christ, the first Greek Gentiles to be appointed to special
duties, along with the apostles, were seven in number.
They were to help the disciples to distribute bread to their
own people (Acts 6:1 ff.).

This group at the second feeding was the first gathering of those outside the fold of Judaism to be called to
new life. They were fed with the seven loaves, and when
the fragments were collected after the meal, there were
seven large baskets left, enough for the eternal feeding of
the seventy nations. It is significant that Mark used different words for the baskets in the two incidents. In the

first feeding he used a word meaning something like
"creel," and in the second, the reference is to a much
larger vessel, more like a "hamper." For indeed, much
more bread would be necessary to feed those from the
four corners of the world, the Gentile hordes, than to feed
little Israel.

A Sign from Heaven

As soon as Jesus and the disciples had dismissed the
crowd and again crossed the sea, they were approached by
Pharisees who began to argue with Jesus, seeking a sign
from heaven in order to test him. The passage appears to
be an indirect reference to Deut. 13:2 ff., concerning a
prophet who can produce signs and persuade people to
"leave the way in which the LORD your God commanded
you to walk." Such a prophet was to be put to death. There
can be little doubt about what the Pharisees thought about
Jesus' teaching. He had thrown out the oral law and
severely criticized the written law as being contrary to God's
law, and he had taught his followers likewise. He was
surely a prophet who was persuading his followers to
leave the "right" way, at least in the eyes of the Pharisees.

Jesus showed no intention of being drawn into a trap,
but exhibited sorrow when he asked, "Why does this generation [i.e., group derived from a certain genealogy[35]]
seek a sign?" (Mark 8:12). Then he stated that no sign
would be given to such a group; they would be given no
magic signal concerning the Kingdom of God. Their own
hardness of heart and lack of understanding barred them
from access to that Kingdom. So saying, he and the disciples left and crossed the sea once again.

The One Loaf

Although there was one loaf of bread in the boat, Mark
says that the disciples had forgotten to bring bread. At this

point they were warned by Jesus to "beware of the leaven of the Pharisees and the leaven of Herod" (v. 15). The Pharisees were those who trusted and served that which was other than God—the law. The Herodians, likewise, trusted that which was other than God—the secular forces of the world, in this case, Rome. As the Israelites had complained in the wilderness that they had no bread, so the disciples discussed the fact that they, in their exodus, had no bread. Jesus chided them because of their lack of understanding. They were asked why they discussed the fact that they had no bread. Were they not yet able to perceive or understand, even after the lesson of the feedings? They had not really seen or heard, nor had they remembered. After the Children of Israel had been fed, there were twelve creels of remainders, and after the mixed multitude had been admitted to the table of the Lord, there were seven hampers of bread left. There was scarcely need to worry that they would be fed. Yet they did not understand that there was enough life-bread for all of Israel, plus the rest of the nations.

The apparent meaning of the one loaf is that the twelve and the seven remaining baskets of bread need not be present in the new exodus; only *one* loaf is necessary, and that one loaf with them in the boat is Jesus Christ. He is the unifying principle capable of reconciling mankind to the creation and to God, the Creator. There were twelve whole loaves in the feeding narratives, and one loaf in the boat; i.e., there were thirteen loaves, but Jesus Christ was the replacement for the twelve loaves of the bread of the presence on the altar. He *is* the bread of the presence, the only necessary bread for the sustenance of the new Israel, the loaf spoken of at the Last Supper, the one loaf broken for the world. He is the "bread of life," the right understanding, which can unite man and God in a whole relationship. Those who followed his way, Jew or Gentile, would eat to the full.

The Blind Man of Bethsaida

Mark writes that when Jesus and the disciples reached Bethsaida, Jesus was approached by a group who came begging him to touch a blind man. The story of the healing of the blind man is Mark's symbolic way of describing how difficult it was for the disciples to grasp the understanding of life that Jesus was offering them. Again, Mark says that Jesus spat, this time on the man's blind eyes, and laid hands on him. A little understanding was beginning to dawn on the new Israel, for when the blind man was asked if he could see anything, he confessed that he could see dimly, but as yet incorrectly. "I see men; but they look like trees, walking." (Ch. 8:24.) The difficulty of the cure is emphasized when Mark states that Jesus repeated his touch, a repetition without parallel in the Gospel. The man looked "intently"—the disciples were putting a great deal of will and endeavor into trying to see, to *understand* correctly. That they were at least partially successful is attested to by the very next conversation between them and Jesus.

Peter's Confession

When the man had been dismissed, Mark says that Jesus and the disciples went on their way. Jesus began to test the actual level of understanding that the disciples had reached, and asked them how people regarded him. They replied that he was commonly regarded as a resurrected John or Elijah, or some other of the prophets. Then Jesus put them to the supreme test, "But who do you say that I am?" At last he was rewarded with a flicker of recognition. "Peter answered him, 'You are the Christ.'" (V. 29.)

With Peter's confession Mark demonstrates a recognition of Jesus as one who indeed was engaged in a special way in revealing God's will for man, even though Peter and the disciples subsequently, and throughout the remainder of the Gospel, exhibited no real comprehension of the nature of that will. That Peter's recognition was indeed a mere flash of understanding is verified by Jesus' revelation of the ultimate suffering and death of the Christ, to which Peter responded with a rebuke. This was the first of three predictions of the crucifixion (chs. 8:31; 9:31; 10:33). In each, Jesus stated in increasing detail the events of the week in Jerusalem.

The disciples were clearly not able to absorb the meaning of Peter's confession. They were seeing, but not clearly. Jesus, realizing their lack of understanding, addressed a counter rebuke to Peter, which was clearly intended for them all: "Get behind me, Satan! For you are not on the side of God, but of men." (Ch. 8:33.) The disciples apparently harbored some of the same messianic expectations as the populace at large, and could not conceive that their teacher would soon be taken from them.

After each of the three predictions of Christ's suffering and death, Mark leaves no doubt in the reader's mind of the fact that the disciples had no idea of what their affirmative answer to Jesus' "Follow me" represented in the way of commitment. As Leander Keck so aptly puts it in an article on Mark, "The disciples trail Jesus but neither 'follow' nor understand what 'following' really means."[36] After each passion prediction the teaching of Jesus is an attempt to enlighten them as to the real meaning of their following him to become God's covenanted people. To understand with his understanding meant, first of all, self-forgetfulness. It meant assuming the burdens of other people's lives, an assumption expressed in a life of loving service to fellowman. It meant to become completely "other-directed" in the sense that the welfare of others becomes one's primary life concern, at whatever cost in personal suffering and tribulation. The life of service to others was not to be regarded as one of degradation and shame—it is the only *authentic* life, and self-aggrandizement has no place in the Kingdom of God.

When Mark's Jesus predicted that there were among those present some who would witness the coming of the Kingdom of God with power, it cannot be denied that this actually happened, for with the acceptance of the new self-understanding brought to these followers, and those who in turn followed them, in truth the Kingdom of God, as depicted by Mark, came into being. Lives were changed from empty obeisance to the law, and released into meaningful relationship to God and neighbor. The true meaning of entering the Kingdom of God, which is everywhere and at all times at hand, is to give one's life over to the loving and serving of one's fellowman.

Summary

The narratives of the feedings, interspersed with the crossing of the sea, the discussion of the Pharisaical, i.e., literal, interpretation of the law, the two healing incidents, the discussion of the sign, and the one loaf, are all of a piece. There is first a Jewish feeding narrative, followed by Jesus' temptation (walking on the water) to pass by the Israelite remnant because of its hardness of heart, i.e., its lack of understanding of the function of the chosen people. Then, the only Gentile healing narrative is inserted and is couched in terms of feeding and eating.

After the Gentiles had been made whole and accepted into the covenant (symbolized in the Gentile healing), even if only after the original children themselves had been fed, the narration of the Gentile feeding follows. The original children were fed with their five loaves, leaving a remainder of twelve baskets for eternal food, and the Gentiles had been invited to the table and fed with the seven loaves, leaving a remainder of seven baskets as promise for eternal sustenance.

Perceiving the revelation of God's covenant, Israel should have opened her ears to hear God's commands, and her tongue, released from its fetters, should have been able to speak to the world of God's reconciling love. Not only did the Pharisees, the leaders of Israel, fail to perceive the truth, but the disciples themselves were uncomprehending, and had not realized either the composition of the Kingdom or that it was at hand. The bread of life was with them, but how long would new Israel's blindness and infirmity to God's will continue?

The extra loaf is the only loaf left, and is all that is needed for the new exodus, for it is the bread of life provided by God and manifested in Jesus Christ. Those who follow his way will eat to the full and not from remaining fragments. Those who eat of the bread of true life are those who live lives of love and commitment, lives of realized fulfillment.

Chapter 7

THE NEW LAWGIVER
AND PROPHET

Mark 9:2 to 10:31

The Transfiguration

FOLLOWING PETER'S RECOGNITION of Jesus as the
Christ, and Jesus' teaching of what it meant to follow the
Christ in the covenant with God, Mark says that "after six
days Jesus took with him Peter and James and John, and
led them up a high mountain apart by themselves; and he
was transfigured before them, and his garments became
glistening, intensely white, as no fuller on earth could
bleach them" (ch. 9:2). When Moses had taken the
seventy elders up Sinai to witness God's glory, he had
taken with him three disciples, Aaron, Nadab, and Abihu.
They gathered together on the mountain in the presence
of God's glory. Then God told Moses to go farther up on
the mountain so that he might receive the tablets of God's
commandments. The glory of God covered the mountain
for six days, and *after six days* God called to Moses out of
the cloud, and the glory of the Lord was "like a devouring
fire on the top of the mountain" (Ex. 24:15 ff.).

While the two mountains, that in Exodus and that in
Mark, are not the same, Mark's mountain symbolizes
Sinai, the meeting place with God, where men were called
and where they agreed to the covenant with God. God
revealed himself to Moses and to Elijah on a mountain.
Jesus had instituted the Twelve as the new Israel on a

"mountain," and here he and the three disciples were joined by Moses and Elijah, the symbols of the Law and the Prophets. Peter, carried away by awe and fright, suggested that they build three booths (tabernacles), one each for Jesus, Moses, and Elijah. That Mark enters the suggestion of "tabernacles" at this point should not be surprising, for the first portion of the discourse between Moses and God during Moses' forty days on the mountain concerned God's command that the people should build for him a Tabernacle that he might dwell in their midst. Peter desired to prolong the experience, but to do so would have been to misunderstand the significance of the episode as Mark has related it. The voices of Moses and Elijah were not to be associated with the voice of Jesus, nor were they to remain as the supreme guiding lights for the new Israel. Mark says a voice from the cloud established the one true spiritual guide of the new Israel: "This is my beloved Son; listen to him" (ch. 9:7). So Mark dramatizes the fulfillment of the Old Testament, for in Deut. 18:15, Moses had told the people, "The LORD your God will raise up for you a prophet like me from among you, from your brethren—him you shall heed." And God had said to Moses: "I will raise up for them a prophet like you from among their brethren; and I will put my words in his mouth, and he shall speak to them all that I commanded him. And whoever will not give heed to my words which he shall speak in my name, I myself will require it of him." (Vs. 18 f.)

As Mark symbolically replaced the priests with Jesus (see Chapter 3), and substituted Jesus for the bread of the presence (see Chapter 6), so Jesus and his teaching become in Mark the replacement for and transcendence of the Law and the Prophets. Moses and Elijah fade away, "And suddenly looking around they no longer saw any one with them but Jesus only" (Mark 9:8). Jesus alone remained as the symbol of God's presence and reconciling word, and the disciples were commanded to heed him.

The occasion on the mountain in the Old Testament was the giving of God's law to the people. Moses was to become responsible for their obedience to the law entrusted to him. As God's law had come to old Israel in a former time, an equivalent time would be a necessity in the new exodus. In Mark's exodus, the old law and its proponent, prophecy, passed away, and those making up the new Israel were commanded not to renew themselves under the old law but to heed Jesus. He became, in Mark, the new lawgiver and the new prophet, imbued with God's own Spirit. Peter's confession received divine affirmation on the mountain. Jesus is affirmed as God's Son, replacing all other symbols of God's presence, i.e., the professional priesthood, the bread of God's presence, the lawgiver, and the prophets. That the new exodus is to be in no way related to a popular revolution under a Davidic messiah has also been made clear. The new exodus is to new life, and new life cannot come into being without the death of the old, "for whoever would save his life will lose it" (Mark 8:35).

After presenting the transfiguration, Mark then clarifies once and for all that John the Baptist is the returned Elijah alluded to in ch. 1:2 ff. Malachi 4:5 f. proclaimed the coming of the herald, Elijah *cum* John the Baptist. It was he who was to come "before the great and terrible day of the LORD comes. And he will turn the hearts of fathers to their children and the hearts of children to their fathers, lest I come and smite the land with a curse." Elijah/John had come and met his Jezebel in Herodias, and died by the sword as Jezebel had vowed of Elijah (I Kings 19: 1 ff.). The Son of Man has come, and he will suffer as was prophesied in Isaiah and The Psalms.

The Boy with a Dumb Spirit

After Jesus and the disciples came down from the mountain and joined the other disciples, they were confronted by a father concerned for his child. He had brought his son to Jesus, but finding only the disciples, had asked them for healing of the child from his affliction, believing, apparently, that being followers of Jesus they likewise possessed his spirit. Their inability to effect a cure exacted a rebuke from Jesus concerning the lack of faith residing in this remnant called out of Israel.

The writer of Deuteronomy says that Moses finished writing all the Books of the Law and immediately prior to his death commanded the Levites to place them next to the Ark of the Covenant as a witness. Moses prophesied that after his death there would be a rebellion of the stubborn people against "the way" in which he had commanded them to walk. They were rebellious while he was yet alive; how much more corrupt they would be after his death! They would surely do evil in the sight of the Lord, moving him to anger through the work of their hands.

Jesus' words to the disciples are very much like those of Moses in his final song to Israel, for when Jesus rebuked the disciples, he called them a faithless generation:

A God of faithfulness and without iniquity,
  just and right is he.
They have dealt corruptly with him,
  they are no longer his children because of their blemish;
  they are a perverse and crooked generation.

(Deut. 32:4 f.)

New Israel bore the blemishes of the old, and as a result its members were seized by a spirit that rendered them helpless and incapable of keeping the covenant and imparting the good news, a spirit of self-understanding that indeed contained the seed of self-destruction. Jesus asked that the boy be brought to him, whereupon, when confronted by Jesus, Mark says the child was immediately seized by a spirit which was described by the father as one of long standing, desirous of destroying the child. " 'How long has he had this?' . . . 'From childhood. And it has often cast him into the fire and into the water, to destroy him; but if you can do anything, have pity on us and help us.' " (Ch. 9:21 f.) Jesus' response was in essence one close to derision, reiterating with emphasis, "If you *can!*" The man was told that all things were possible to one who believed; i.e., one can live in the way to which he has been called by the Christ if one only believes truly that that is the way commanded by God.

Mark seems to be saying the following with this narrative: Israel wanted to believe. There was something compelling in the spirit of the man Jesus, who had become her leader, which called her to decision, to believe his way to be God's way, to be healed, to be delivered from the seizures of rebellion which had many times threatened to destroy Israel of old, to be capable of a witness that would not appear to be foaming nonsense at the mouth or grinding teeth in the search for truth and understanding. "I believe; help my unbelief!" It was the father who spoke, but his statement symbolized the residual of disbelief and reluctance to total commitment evidenced in the new Israel. When that unclean spirit, which kept Israel from a whole relationship to God, was rebuked by Jesus, he commanded it to come out, and the deaf and dumb spirit was never to enter into the body again.

It was not an easy cure. The wrench of cutting oneself off from the familiar, from tradition, from the comfort and the safety of obedience to a way of life completely circumscribed by the law, which removed from one the call to decision and self-responsibility, was not an easy separation. When Israel at last committed herself to following the way of the Christ, and felt the terrible wrench of her separation from the old, she appeared, as we see in the symbolism of Mark's narrative, as one who had passed from life to death. " 'He is dead.' But Jesus . . . lifted him up, and he arose." (Vs. 26 f.) When the spirit of self-understanding that resided in Jesus motivated Israel, she could arise.

This is the last healing in Mark of those who were incapable of hearing and speaking. Israel's ears and tongue have been healed and placed in the service of God's covenant. If only she can be made to *see,* to perceive, to understand, she can become the instrument of God's love for the world.

Leaving Galilee

Teaching them as they journeyed, Jesus and the disciples passed quietly through Galilee. Jesus' teaching concerned the second prediction of his death and resurrection. The disciples did not understand, and Mark says that they were afraid to ask about it. Perhaps Mark's implication is that they had been intimidated by Jesus' impatience at their previous lack of understanding. On the journey, which ended at Capernaum, they were involved in a discussion among themselves. When asked by Jesus of the nature of the discussion they held their silence, for they had discussed with one another which of them was the greatest. Aware of their misapprehension of the nature of the Kingdom of God, Jesus called them to him. He placed a child in their midst, and then taking the child in his arms tells them, "Whoever receives one such child in my name receives me; and whoever receives me, receives not me but him who sent me" (v. 27), a repetition, in a different form, of his earlier admonition that those who would follow in his way must be willing to forget self in the service of others, even the least, even a little child, for had not Isaiah said, "A little child shall lead them" (Isa. 11:6)? And should they find someone following the way, preaching the good news, but not as one of their members, they were not to take offense and attempt to exclude that person from the Kingdom. All who follow the way of service and self-forgetfulness do so in the name of the understanding of the Christ, God's Word of love and reconciliation. All are to be welcomed. The individual who does even so tiny a deed as giving a cup of water in the service of fellowman in the spirit of God's love is himself a member of the Kingdom of God.

While the disciples were discussing among themselves the subject of "Who is the greatest?" they had missed Jesus' discourse on the necessity of the suffering of the servant of God. A servant is one who loses his life, not one who argues over rank. Whatever it is in a man's life that causes him to place regard for self above concern for fellowman is a breach in the wholeness of the relationship between man and God, whether it be preservation of self, or preservation of one's possessions, as is shortly explored in the encounter with the rich young man.

Following the private teaching at Capernaum, the company left and made its way to the region of Judea and beyond the Jordan. That Mark says they have crossed the Jordan subsequent to the revelation of Jesus' substitution for the first lawgiver, Moses, and for the great prophet Elijah, has great significance,[37] for it was in this area that Moses made his only entry into Israel during the exodus, and it was here that Moses delivered the Books of the Law to the people (Deut. 32:48 ff.). It was here that Moses died, and turned his leadership over to Jesus (Joshua, the son of Nun), and the task of finishing the work which Moses had begun. Now, in the transfiguration, Moses, symbol of law and lawgiver, has again passed from the scene, leaving only Joshua (Jesus of Nazareth) to carry on the work of the covenant. And it was in this same geographical vicinity that Elijah had been taken away, and his mantle passed on to his successor Elisha.

Transcending the Mosaic Law

John, the forerunner, had also left the scene, and according to Mark, his assassination was because of his stand on the marriage of Herod and Herodias. Mark proceeds to depict Jesus calling man to transcend the law of Moses, in this case, the law concerning divorce. When Jesus passed over the Jordan, he was accosted by the Pharisees, who, in order to test him, asked him, "Is it lawful for a man to divorce his wife?" (ch. 10:2). Jesus is portrayed as a new lawgiver and more, for he calls men beyond the law to its spirit. In his reply he changed the law that Moses had given to the people, making it more stringent (because of their hardness of heart). He declared that divorce was not permissible under the law of God, and any who divorce and remarry have committed adultery. While John adhered to tradition, and called the people to repentance and obedience to the Mosaic law, Jesus asserted that that law was insufficient in the eyes of God. It was at the very place where Moses had given the law, cited by the Pharisees, that Jesus overruled it. Again, Mark makes an oblique reference to Isa. 11:6, and points to a child as a leader into the Kingdom of God, for one must accept the Kingdom in the same trusting manner as does a child.

The Rich Young Man

Following the discussion about divorce, Jesus reaffirmed the intent of God's law as stated in the Ten Commandments. When he was approached by a young man requesting the secret of inheriting eternal life, Jesus referred him to the moral law. The man said that he had kept the law

since his youth. The only law with which he was confronted by Jesus was the moral law, and there is no mention made of the ceremonial law or the oral law, i.e., the
tradition of the elders. Jesus told the man he lacked one
thing only, to sell all and "follow the way." This admonition was contrary to the principle of the law that limited
a man's philanthropic impulses to no more than one fifth
of his property. It was likewise contrary to orthodox
Judaism which stated that it was unlawful to give away all
one's possessions.[38] The Old Testament regarded the loss
of one's wealth as evidence of disfavor with God. This is
the entire case Job's friends brought against him. Jesus'
intent is plain, however; neither one's physical well-being
nor his material possessions must be allowed to become
a stumbling block for entering the Kingdom for service
to God and fellowman.

It was no wonder that the disciples were perplexed.
Although they had left all, as Peter so carefully pointed
out to Jesus, they could not comprehend that wealth, a
sign of God's favor, could stand in the way of a man's
entering the Kingdom. They asked, in the face of Jesus'
new teaching, "Who can be saved?" (ch. 10:26). The
lesson they must learn is that "to be saved" means literally
"to live," and it is those who are willing to give up their
lives who will find that they are truly living, and their
reward in the service of God will be not wealth or prestige
but the gift of the family of man as their own family. The
fifth and sixth chapters of Deuteronomy are Moses' sum-
marizing of the law that God had given to Israel, and
contains a warning about those things likely to cause one
to forget God, viz., "When the LORD your God brings you
into the land which he swore to your fathers, . . . to give
you, with great and goodly cities, which you did not build,
and houses full of all good things, which you did not fill,
and cisterns hewn out, which you did not hew, and

vineyards and olive trees, which you did not plant, and when you eat and are full, then take heed lest you forget the LORD, who brought you out of the land of Egypt, out of the house of bondage" (Deut. 6:10 ff.). The young man possessed all those very things which caused him to forget the God who called him to deliverance from bondage. Mere obedience to the law is not enough, only he who is willing to be last in prestige, power, or possessions is fit to be a servant in the Kingdom of God and thereby know true fulfillment of life.

Summary

Mark's Jesus has been revealed as the fulfillment of God's presence and of the prophecies of the old covenant. He has been designated by Mark as the one true leader of the struggling little group of disciples who have been called to be the new Israel, God's servant to call to him all men of however lowly station, of whatever breed, indeed, to borrow a much used contemporary phrase, all men of whatever race, creed, or color. The disciples were still dragging behind Jesus, caught up in their own understanding of what it meant to enter into the Kingdom, unable to take in the real meaning of being the covenanted servant of God in the new exodus. Because they had not understood the meaning of the word of reconciliation and deliverance, they were unable to proclaim it to others, or even truly to see that it must be proclaimed to all others. They continued to vie with one another for favored position, and were jealous when one outside their exclusive little group appeared able to apprehend the spirit of God's love more clearly than they. They were taught by Jesus that they must rid themselves of whatever stood between them and an open relationship to fellowman in the service of God's love. This they must do by dedication and commitment to that service. While their reward was not to be one of wealth, prestige, or favor, it would be an even greater gift, the gift of a life fulfilled by their acceptance into the Kingdom of God.

So ends the ministry in Galilee. Jesus and the disciples turned their steps toward Jerusalem. Confronted with the real meaning of the call to which they had responded, the disciples experienced awe, wonder, and even terror as they walked into the time ahead.

Chapter 8

JERUSALEM

Mark 10:32 to 13:37

The Third Prediction

MARK WRITES THAT as Jesus and the disciples turned toward Jerusalem they carried with them a group of followers, who apparently regarded Jesus with a great deal of wonder and fear. Along the way, for the third time,[39] Jesus took the disciples aside and began to tell them what they must expect in Jerusalem. This time the details were more fully revealed and included the information that the chief priests and the scribes would condemn him to death (which legally, of course, they could not do; it would be necessary to force the Roman authority to carry out their sentence). Typically, Mark dramatizes for his reader the fact that the disciples continued to harbor their own, and incorrect, understanding of Jesus' "Messiahship." James and John asked Jesus to do them the favor of granting them the preferred right- and left-hand seats when Jesus had come into glory. It is not clear from the request, as given, whether the reference to glory is worldly or otherwise, nor, for that matter, is it particularly important. The point is that the disciples were still disputing with one another about personal greatness, power, and prestige.

Again Mark follows such a discussion with a section of teaching, which by now has become formula, delineating the true nature of the call to covenant. When Jesus asked if James and John were able to enter into the kind of "baptism" reserved for him, they affirmed they were, and in turn were assured that they would—persecution, suffering, and martyrdom became the norm for followers of Christ, as Mark very well knew. As a matter of fact, James, the disciple, was martyred under Herod Agrippa, ca. A.D. 41–44, the first of the apostles to be baptized with death. There is a tradition that John suffered the same fate. James and John were also told that Jesus had no authority to grant "rank."

Following the request, Mark related the indignant reaction of the remaining ten disciples, presumably the two had gone behind their backs to gain extra favor with their leader. Once again, all were called and taught what was involved in being a follower of the Christ. For the first time in Mark, Jesus referred to authority over the Gentiles, but Mark phrased the statement in such a way that it can have a double interpretation; e.g. (1) those of new Israel were not to pattern their authority as teachers on the behavior of secular authorities over the Gentiles; or (2) when the Twelve carried the message to the Gentiles, they were to do so as servants, not in a condescending manner, but as slaves, for the Son of Man himself came only to serve. He came, *not* to be a ruler or an authoritarian lord, but a servant willing to give his life for the lowliest, so that in turn new life might become a gift for all. Mark would most certainly have known of the arrogance of the Jewish rulers, particularly those in Jerusalem, and the manner in which they treated Gentile converts in the mission churches; e.g., at Antioch they refused to eat with "unclean" Gentiles (Gal. 2:11 ff.). If Mark had merely wished to draw a contrast between arrogant rule and servanthood, he could have used as an example the rulers of Israel. Rather it would appear from Mark that Jesus desired to teach the disciples directly concerning their demeanor when they carried the gospel to the Gentiles.

Jericho and the Blind Beggar

As the company made their way to Jerusalem and came to Jericho, they were confronted by Bartimaeus, the blind beggar.[40] This is the final healing narrative in the Gospel, the previous one having dealt with hearing and speaking. The immediately preceding discourse on the meaning of discipleship was precipitated by the "blindness" of James and John. New Israel is still not able to perceive the true nature of her call to service, and must be healed of all blindness that blocks her understanding. Bartimaeus, upon hearing that it was Jesus of Nazareth (i.e., a shoot from Jesse and therefore of the lineage of David) passing by, called out, "Jesus, Son of David, have mercy on me!" (ch. 10:47). When the crowd attempted to silence him (we are not told why), he cried all the more. Jesus, without disclaiming the title at this particular time, called the man to him. Bartimaeus was asked by Jesus, in exactly the same words he had put to James and John above, "What do you want me to do for you?" (v. 51). James and John had requested not only that which Jesus stated was not within his province to grant but more yet, something irrelevant to any participant of the new exodus. They had not asked for "sight," although that was the gift of healing Jesus had offered them with his teaching, notwithstanding which they apparently remained blind. The words of Jeremiah are called to mind: "Declare this in the house of Jacob, proclaim it in Judah: 'Hear this, O foolish and senseless people, who have eyes, but see not, who have ears, but hear not' " (Jer. 5:20 f.). To one who asked for sight, even though he addressed Jesus by a title that had all the connotations of the sort of "popular messiah" implied in the understanding of James and John, the request was willingly granted. Bartimaeus was told to go on his way. Now that Bartimaeus had received his sight, Jesus' way became his way, and he followed after Jesus.

The Entry

The way brought the company closer to Jerusalem, and as they came nearer, Jesus sent two of the disciples into the village to fetch a colt on which no one had sat (ch. 11:1 ff.). The entire passage is not only steeped in symbolism and unveiled references to the Old Testament, but, in the fashion of Mark's writing, is capable of supporting a double interpretation by its very nature, i.e., the understanding of the role expected of Jesus by the crowd, and the contrasting understanding he had been attempting to convey to his disciples. There are three Old Testament references in the background of the passage. The first is Gen. 49:10, which is the prophecy of Jacob concerning the future inheritance of his twelve sons. Because of the treachery of Reuben, Simeon, and Levi, Judah, Jacob's fourth son by Leah, received the birthright ordinarily bestowed on the firstborn. Judah was, through Perez, the ancestor of David (Ruth 4:18 ff.). The prophecy of Jacob declares that Judah would, of all the twelve sons (tribes), be at the head, and the eleven would bow down before him. The scepter and ruler's staff would belong to Judah "until he comes to whom it belongs; and to him shall be the obedience of the peoples. Binding his foal to the vine and his ass's colt to the choice vine" (Gen. 49:10 f.). (Matthew says that Jesus sent for an ass and a colt, and then rode on both of them "to fulfil what was spoken by the prophet," Matt. 21:4.)

The second Old Testament reference concerns Solomon's ascension to the throne soon to be vacated by his ailing father, David. David ordered that Solomon his son should ride on David's own mule to Gihon where he was to be anointed as king over Israel. It was so done. Zadok the priest took the horn of oil and anointed Solomon; the trumpet blew, and the people cried, "Long live King Solomon!" (I Kings 1:39). They went up after him, playing on pipes, rejoicing, and making a great noise. This is a picture of the triumphal procession of a secular king, anointed to rule over Israel when she was at the height of her worldly glory.

The third Old Testament passage is that referred to by Matthew, Zech. 9:9, which is an oracle placed after a declaration from the Lord to Jerusalem (Judah), telling her of God's good intentions for her. Not only will she come into joy and gladness, but many peoples shall come from many cities to seek the Lord of Hosts in Jerusalem. "In those days ten men from the nations of every tongue shall take hold of the robe of a Jew, saying, 'Let us go with you, for we have heard that God is with you.'" (Zech. 8:23.) The oracle that follows is chiefly a diatribe against the traditional enemies of Israel and a prediction of their downfall. After the oppressors have been dealt with, Israel is to shout aloud and rejoice, for "lo, your king comes to you; triumphant and victorious is he, humble and riding on an ass, on a colt the foal of an ass" (Zech. 9:9). The oracle states that the one who comes, though he comes victoriously, comes also humbly, not as a warrior, but upon a beast that symbolizes a nation at peace, and he will command peace to the nations, an association of ideas more closely akin to the teaching of Jesus to his disciples than to their interpretation by or the expectations of the multitude of followers.

When the colt had been brought, garments were thrown upon it and Jesus sat upon it. Garments and leafy branches cut from the fields (Ps. 118:26 f.) were spread on the road. Those who accompanied Jesus into the city shouted: "Hosanna! Blessed is he who comes in the name of the

Lord! Blessed is the kingdom of our father David that is coming! Hosanna in the highest!" (Mark 11:9 f.) Bartimaeus had called Jesus "Son of David," and the crowd referred to the kingdom he brought as from "our father David." In either case, the association of Jesus with the role of a Davidic messiah is one that illustrates the chasm between the understanding of the populace, presumably including the disciples, and the picture Jesus himself painted of his role.

Upon entering Jerusalem they went to the Temple. Jesus made what appears to be, from Mark's description, a thorough investigation of it, after which they retired to Bethany.

The Cursing of the Fig Tree

The following morning on their way back to Jerusalem from Bethany, Mark states that Jesus was hungry, and seeing a fig tree in leaf went to see if there was anything on it. But when he came to it, he found nothing but leaves (for it was not the season for figs), and he said to it, "May no one ever eat fruit from you again" (ch. 11:14).

The Cleansing of the Temple

The cleansing of the Temple falls between the two halves of the story of the cursed and withered fig tree. After Jesus entered Jerusalem, he went to the Temple and began to drive out those who bought and sold sacrificial animals, and he overturned the tables of the money changers. The scene of Jesus' violent action, the only such related by Mark, is generally believed to be the "court of the Gentiles or heathen,"[41] that portion of the Temple set aside for Gentile worship.

The court of the Gentiles was separated by a high partitioning wall from the holier parts of the Temple, and the court itself was regarded as having little sacred significance. It was a wide enclosure giving access to the interior parts of the building, but it was part of the Temple, and as such, fell under certain regulations. No one was to pass through it with dusty feet, or use it as a thoroughfare, and the use of it by the sick was forbidden. Because it was convenient and quite large, the sale of sacrificial beasts was licensed and allowed by the high priest, as was the exchanging of Roman coins of the worshipers for Temple shekels, the only acceptable mint for annual tribute, etc. There seems little doubt that this was a profitable business for the chief priest, but it was, nevertheless, a great convenience to the traveler, faced with the necessity, otherwise, of hauling sacrificial animals with him.

The buying and selling of sacrificial animals was not inherently evil, and it was not merely the commerce that was attacked by Jesus. Note that Mark says he "would not allow any one to carry anything through the temple" (ch. 11:16); i.e., he would not allow the use of the court for a shortcut. He was opposing the misuse of this court.

Jesus' words concerning the Temple, "My house shall be called a house of prayer for all the nations . . . but you have made it a den of robbers," must be seen in their Old Testament context (Isa. 56:7). Not only were all nations called to worship God, Isaiah goes on to say:

And the foreigners who join themselves to the LORD,
    to minister to him, to love the name of the LORD,
    and to be his servants,
every one who keeps the sabbath, and does not profane it,
    and holds fast my covenant—
these I will bring to my holy mountain,
    and make them joyful in my house of prayer;
their burnt offerings and their sacrifices
    will be accepted on my altar;
for my house shall be called a house of prayer
    for all peoples.
Thus says the Lord GOD,

who gathers the outcasts of Israel,
I will gather yet others to him
besides those already gathered.

(Vs. 6 ff.)

Jesus claimed that the priests had made the Temple of the Lord a den of thieves, i.e., the priests had stolen for themselves the right of the Gentiles to know God. Isaiah 56:11 states that the "dogs [God's watchmen] have a mighty appetite; they never have enough. The shepherds also have no understanding; they have all turned to their own way, each to his own gain, one and all."

Mark alone of the Synoptists completes the quotation from Isaiah, "My house shall be called a house of prayer," with "for all nations." Jesus' violent action and verbal chastisement dealt exclusively with the rights of the Gentiles. He did not in any way interfere with Jewish ritual or worship. Conversely, his apparent ignoring of the exclusive Jewish worship and sacrifice which occupied the balance of the Temple would almost seem to say that the function of the priesthood was no longer an important concern. His claim, however, was that the whole Temple had been desecrated by the corruption of the outer court. He was intent upon removing from it the commercial traffic that interfered with the worship of the Gentiles, for it was prophesied in Zechariah, when the day of the Lord arrived, when all the families of the earth worshiped God in his holy house, "there shall no longer be a trader in the house of the Lord of hosts on that day" (Zech. 14:21). It is apparent from the disrespectful use to which this court was put that the priesthood did not take very seriously the injunction that the Temple was to be a house of prayer and worship for all nations. "For the sons of Judah have done evil in my sight, says the Lord; they have set their abominations in the house which is called by my name, to defile it." (Jer. 7:30.)

Jesus' teaching was greeted by the people with astonishment. Mark used this word four other times, and each time the amazement is linked directly with the *difference* between the teaching of Jesus and that of the scribes. When the priests and the scribes sought a way to destroy him, their action was attributed by Mark not to the rough action of Jesus but rather to his teaching. It was what Jesus taught in the Temple which offended, the thought and reason for his act of violence, and not merely the deed, which led them to seek a way to destroy him, a reaction identical to that of the Pharisees and the Herodians in the synagogue at Galilee on the occasion of the restoration of the withered hand (Mark 3:6).

The Withered Fig Tree

After teaching in the Temple, Jesus and the disciples left the city in the evening. The following morning as they passed by, they saw the cursed fig tree "withered away to its roots." It was Peter who remembered the incident of the previous day. He said: "Master, look! The fig tree which you cursed has withered." (Mark 11:31.)

Before our study proceeds with an interpretative discussion of the incident, the symbolism of "fig tree" should be considered. The tree, which is native to western Asia, was highly prized and is often mentioned in the Old Testament along with the vine (Deut. 8:8; Ps. 105:33; Jer. 5:17; Joel 1:12). To sit under one's vine and one's fig tree was the symbol of prosperity and security (I Kings 4:25). The tree/vine and their fruits were a common symbol for the nation, Israel (Isa. 5:1 ff.; Jer. 8:13; Micah 7:1), but to invite the nations under the shelter of the branches of Israel's fig tree is a figurative statement referring to the Temple, which was to be a shelter of God's love for the world. The Temple had been exposed as barren of such fruits, and the fig tree, the symbolic equiva-

lent for the Temple, like the Temple, was withered away
to its roots.

If the fig tree (the rulers of the Temple, and therefore,
the Temple itself) was withered away to its roots, how
could Israel invite her neighbors under the shelter of her
vine and her fig tree? (Zech. 3:10). Israel had no shelter
and no food to offer her neighbors, the nations. Her
branches, watered by God's reconciling love, were meant
to be a shelter for all the world, and the fruit of her word
was to feed the world. The old branch was withered, and
a new branch must replace her. "Behold, the man whose
name is the Branch" (Zech. 6:12)—Jesus is the new
branch come to offer God's sheltering love to the world.

Yet Mark carefully called attention to the fact that it
was not the season for figs; why then should Jesus arbi-
trarily curse it? But had it ever been the season for fruit
with Israel? It was never the right season for bearing fruit.
The priesthood was not even concerned to preserve an
outside court of the Temple for the admission of the nations, much less to gather them in for the Kingdom of
God. Just like Jonah, her Tabernacle was for her own
benefit. Old Israel thought there was no right season for
proclaiming the gospel, and did not even understand what
fruit it was that God expected her to bring forth. "You
will know them by their fruits" (Matt. 7:16), but Israel
had not borne any fruit. She had, instead, under her corrupt leadership, lived a barren life, shut up within herself, coveting the Temple for her own shelter, cut off
from the hated unclean world to which she had been sent
by God as servant to call all men to him. "When I would
gather them, says the LORD, there are no grapes on the
vine, nor figs on the fig tree; even the leaves are withered,
and what I gave them has passed away from them." (Jer.
8:13.) What God had given Israel, the covenant to be a
servant to the world, Mark has symbolically removed with

Jesus' cursing of the fig tree and its subsequent withering. "May no one ever eat fruit from you again." (Mark 11:14.)

In an earlier episode in Mark, with many ties to this passage, Jesus had restored the withered hand in the synagogue (ch. 3:1 ff.). The scribes and the Pharisees, disapproving of healing on the Sabbath, were given the choice of favoring the giving of life or the taking of life. They had chosen death, and then sought a way to destroy Jesus. In the Temple it was they who were condemned by Jesus, and the sign of their death was the withering of the fig tree. In the story of the withered hand in the Old Testament (I Kings 13:1 ff.), with which the above episode was compared (see Chapter 3), the corrupt altars of a mercenary priesthood were overturned. Mark's Jesus turned over the mercenary altars (money tables) of the corrupt priesthood and placed the corrupt priesthood itself under the sign of death.

Having found the Temple a barren place, instead of a house of prayer built on faith, Jesus spoke to the disciples of prayer and faith on their way back to Jerusalem. When they came again to the Temple, Jesus was confronted by the chief priests, the scribes, and the elders, and the last discourse with the hierarchy took place.

The New Law and the New Prophecy

When Jesus and his disciples reentered Jerusalem and went to the Temple, they were confronted by the chief priests, the scribes, and the elders demanding to know by what authority Jesus performed his acts. Mark has from the beginning of his book established that authority for his reader. The closest companions of Jesus have developed from a total ignorance of that authority to a slowly dawning recognition of its source. And while Jesus' rejoinder to the Temple officials may appear rather adolescent to a sophisticated modern reader, Mark's intention is clear. There would surely have been no profit in a straightforward answer. While on the face of it Jesus' question appears to parry the inquiry, it is, in truth, an answer to the question put to him, for the priests must make the same decision about the authority for Jesus' acts as for John's baptism. If they understand the source of that authority to be God, then the question becomes, Why do they not believe him and follow him? If they say he is merely an eccentric, a fanatic acting on his own behalf and beliefs, they must face the ire of the populace who followed him.

Having terminated his conversation with the priests, Jesus began to teach with a parable, but with a great difference. There was nothing hidden or obscure about the meaning of this one. Its meaning was so clear that the Temple officials, having recognized themselves as its target, would have arrested him then and there had they dared. The parable concerns a vineyard (Israel, planted by God: "For the vineyard of the LORD of hosts is the house of Israel, and the men of Judah are his pleasant planting," Isa. 5:7), its tenants (the priesthood), and the many servants (prophets, e.g., Isaiah, Jeremiah, Micah, Hosea, Amos, etc.) who had called for the fruit of the vineyard for the owner (God), only to be beaten and cast out time and again. The last servant sent by God to gather the harvest (John the Baptist) they had killed, but God had one additional to send, a beloved Son (Jesus), whom he sent because he reasoned they would respect the Son. But instead, they decided to kill the Son and claim the vineyard as their own private property. The parable ends with the warning that the tenants will be destroyed by God and the vineyard given to others (new Israel) with a new leader (Jesus).

When the chief priests were unable to arrest Jesus, they contrived to entrap him with words by sending various groups to him with questions that they might have an excuse to seize him. Mark's recital of the entire sequence of events—the malicious attitude of the jealous priesthood toward Jesus, whose sole desire was to make Israel, old or new, the dedicated instrument of God's will; the trick questions and the feverish search for some excuse, some gimmick if necessary, to seize Jesus and rid themselves of him; (and since there need be no fear of giving away the plot), the final intrigue of the arrest and the trumped-up charges against him—is almost a blow-by-blow reproduction of the last few chapters of the book of The Acts, but there it is Paul who is the protagonist. In the end of The Acts, it was the accident of Paul's Roman citizenship which saved him from a death contrived by the Sanhedrin at Jerusalem.

Mark's Jesus managed to rebut the questions put to him by the Pharisees and the Sadducees, who represented the conspiracy of the Temple priests. Finally, starting at ch. 12:28, Mark substantiates his exaltation of Jesus as the new lawgiver and, a few verses later, the new prophet. When one of the scribes asked which was the supreme commandment, he was rewarded with the new law that transcends the old:

> The first is, "Hear, O Israel: The Lord our God, the Lord is one; and you shall love the Lord your God with all your heart, and with all your soul, and with all your mind, and with all your strength." The second is this, "You shall love your neighbor as yourself." There is no other commandment greater than these.
>
> (Vs. 29 ff.)

With the giving of the greatest commandments, Jesus has taken the place of Moses, and is the new lawgiver for Israel.

Following the giving of Jesus' law, Mark turns back to consideration of Bartimaeus' greeting to Jesus, "Son of David," and sets the record straight in that regard. The

Christ is not the son of David, but rather the son of man
—Adam—who exercises the authority claimed for him
by Daniel (ch. 7), i.e., the Son of Man to whom God had
given dominion over all things (Gen. 1:26). Jesus the
Christ is the new Adam, the beginning again, the source
of a new creation and a new life.

After a brief condemnation of vanity, arrogance, and
hypocrisy, and the example and approval of the humble
sincerity of the gift of the widow to the Temple, Mark
turns to Jesus in his role of new prophet. Much has been
written about the oracle in ch. 13, so much in fact that
there is little value in a detailed discussion of it. The obvious debt Mark owes to Daniel, Jeremiah, Ezekiel, and
Zechariah cannot be gainsaid. The style and content of
the warnings of disaster are closely patterned on the oracle
in the three concluding chapters of Zechariah, although
the content of the prophecy is really more indebted to the
entire prophecy of Jeremiah. All that Mark borrowed,
however, most definitely bears the stamp of his own original creative touch. The reference to the coming of the
Son of Man in clouds is borrowed from Daniel. The promise that the disciples need not be anxious concerning their
testimony before councils, etc., is the same promise made
to Moses by God before he went to convince the Israelites
in Egypt that they must covenant with God in an exodus
to new life. "Who has made man's mouth? Who makes
him dumb, or deaf, or seeing, or blind? Is it not I, the
LORD? Now therefore go, and I will be with your mouth
and teach you what you shall speak." (Ex. 4:11 f.) As
for when the end will come, the disciples were told no
more than Daniel. The words were "shut up and sealed
until the time of the end" (Dan. 12:9), and while the
wicked will not understand, the wise will watch and wait.
The ending of the oracle is particularly interesting. "Watch
therefore . . . lest he come suddenly and find you asleep.
And what I say to you I say to all: Watch." (Mark

13:35 ff.) It is only a short time later at Gethsemane that the disciples are unable to watch with Jesus, and he comes to them three times and finds them asleep.

Jesus has now become for new Israel the lawgiver and the prophet, as well as the priest and the bread of God's presence. The mood of the Gospel is completely altered from this point onward. There are no more teachings or veiled references to the role of Jesus. As a matter of fact, the final chapters of Mark are the only portion of the Gospel with the sound of straightforward "history," yet it can scarcely be so, for while Mark had access to the "eyewitness" report of Peter, there is much reported to which Peter was not an eyewitness.

Chapter 9

THE BETRAYAL AND THE END

Mark 14:1 to 16:8

Judas Iscariot

THE PLOTTING OF THE CHIEF PRIESTS and the scribes
for the destruction of Jesus went apace in Mark's Gospel,
but they feared taking him at a time when there were so
many tourists in town, many of whom were followers of
Jesus, for Mark had said that the great throng was cap-
tivated by his teaching (ch. 12:37). We are given, after
a description of the sinister plotting, the story of the
anointing of Jesus by the woman with a jar of costly oil.
There was some grumbling among those present at the
extravagance of the gesture, but Mark's Jesus defended
the woman's action, declaring she had anointed him to
prepare him for burial. There are no messianic claims
attached to the passage, simply the reference to Jesus' approaching death, but with the woman's action, Jesus
becomes in fact the "anointed one."

Whether Mark intended to show, in the story of the
woman, motivation for the action of Judas, which appears
to rest on it, he has left us to wonder. It should not be a
surprise, however, that it would be the man named
"Judas," of all the disciples, who betrayed Jesus. For in
Mark's Gospel it could scarcely be any other. To be certain that the reader does not miss the point, Mark carefully designated him as Judas Iscariot. "Iscariot" referred

to the geographical background of Judas, and is generally believed to indicate "Kerioth," a village in the south of Judea.[42] In any event, Judas was the only apostle from Judea, the rest were Galileans.

Judas is the Hellenized version of *Judah*. Any student of the prophets, particularly Isaiah and Jeremiah, will remember the often-used phrase, "And now, O inhabitants of Jerusalem and men of Judah" (Isa. 5:3). The men of Judah were synonymous with the inhabitants of Jerusalem. The entire and dire prophecy of Jeremiah was directed against the house of Israel (although at the time Jeremiah wrote, this was merely poetic) and the house of Judah. "There is revolt among the men of Judah and the inhabitants of Jerusalem. They have turned back to the iniquities of their forefathers, who refused to hear my words; they have gone after other gods to serve them; the house of Israel and the house of Judah have broken my covenant which I made with their fathers." (Jer. 11:9 f.) "What is the sin of the house of Judah? Is it not Jerusalem?" (Micah 1:5.) As was pointed out in Chapter 1, to Mark, Jerusalem was the city of doom, and Judas Iscariot is Mark's symbol for that city. It was not merely a man named Judas Iscariot who betrayed Jesus, it was the city of Jerusalem and its sacrilegious spirit of uncleanness.

The scribes and priests in the city were anxiously plotting the destruction of Jesus. The fact that Mark says that Judas went to the priests is inadvertently to say that the plot was no secret. At least, that would appear to be Mark's intention. The fact that Mark mentions an exchange of money calls for an interesting memory of the first Judah in the Old Testament. He was Israel's (Jacob's) fourth son, and it was he who received his father's birthright, Judea. When Joseph, a son of Israel's old age, was one day sent to seek news of his brothers who were tending the sheep far away, they saw him coming from a distance. They were very jealous of him, and in their hatred they planned to kill him. But Reuben begged them to shed no blood. He persuaded them to cast Joseph into a pit, and secretly planned to rescue him at a later time. In Reuben's absence from the others, Judah asked: "What profit is it if we slay our brother and conceal his blood? Come, let us sell him to the Ishmaelites, and let not our hand be upon him, for he is our brother, our own flesh" (Gen. 37:27). And so Joseph was betrayed by his brothers and sold, at Judah's suggestion, as slave to some passing traders for twenty shekels of silver. Is not Mark suggesting that Judas, like Judah of old, proposes to take profit from fate? Jesus had already been anointed for death, so why not realize a profit therefrom? Judas betrayed Jesus to the priests, and was paid for his part in the betrayal, which apparently was to seek a quiet time and a secluded place where the priests could seize Jesus without arousing the ire of the populace. Jesus, of the lineage of David, would also belong to the tribe of Judah, and like Joseph of old, was betrayed by one of his tribal brothers.

The Last Supper

The first day of Unleavened Bread arrived, the day when the sacrificial lambs were slain in preparation for the Passover meal. Two of the disciples were dispatched to locate the room where the company would celebrate the Passover, and to start preparation for the meal. This account very closely resembles the story of the entry into Jerusalem, when two unnamed disciples were dispatched to get the colt for Jesus. The formula in both instances would lead one to believe that preparations had been made very carefully beforehand. Certainly the secret and mysterious manner in which Mark relates both stories heightens the drama and increases the tension of the occasion. When they found a man carrying a jar of water, a most unusual sight and therefore a useful identifying sign, they were to follow him in order to locate the proper room.

When they came together for the meal on Passover eve (days were reckoned sunset to sunset), Mark's Jesus predicted his betrayal by one of the Twelve, who was there sharing the meal with him. The disciples expressed sorrow and began to ask one after another, "Is it I?" (Mark 14:19). Mark does not reveal the identity of the traitor to the company, as does Matthew. The suicide of Judas is another alteration in the story as told by Matthew, who probably wrote his Gospel near the end of the first century, and almost surely after the fall of Jerusalem. That Judas committed suicide in Matthew's Gospel would be an appropriate comment on Jerusalem's suicidal rebellion against Rome.

Mark describes the Passover meal in very much the same terms as Paul describes the Eucharist, although without the injunction to preserve the tradition as a memorial. The wine is referred to as a symbol of Jesus' blood of the covenant. The passage in Zechariah announcing the coming of the king, triumphant and humble, riding on an ass, states that he shall command peace to the nations and have dominion from sea to sea and the ends of the earth. "As for you also, because of the blood of my covenant with you, I will set your captives free from the waterless pit." (Zech. 9:11.) It was only after the death of Jesus that the disciples came to realize the meaning of his life and teaching; it was only after the shedding of his blood that they were set free from bondage to the law.

Gethsemane

They retired after the Passover meal to the Mount of Olives, and to prepare the disciples for their defection, Mark's Jesus quoted from Zechariah, "Strike the shepherd, that the sheep may be scattered"(Zech. 13:7). Then he told them that the resurrected life they would experience through him would be in Galilee, where he would go to meet them. Even though Peter vehemently denied the possibility of his desertion, and asserted his willingness to die with Jesus, he was told he would desert, nevertheless, denying Jesus three times.

The group went to a place called Gethsemane, a withdrawal which has previously been discussed in Chapter 2. While the disciples had avowed their devotion to Jesus a short time before on the Mount of Olives, the three who went with Jesus to a place apart were not even able to stay awake to watch with him. The night of the Passover, the night before the deliverance from bondage, is known as the "night of watching," and it was incumbent on Israel to keep that "night of watching" throughout their generations (Ex. 12:41 f.). The failure of the disciples to watch over the Lord resembles the story in the Old Testament which relates that David had stolen into the camp of the king, Saul, and could have killed him had he so desired because Abner was asleep. "Why then have you not kept watch over your lord the king? For one of the people came in to destroy the king your lord. The thing that you have done is not good. As the LORD lives, you deserve to die, because you have not kept watch over your lord, the LORD's anointed." (I Sam. 26:15 f.)

The entire scene suggests the words of Ps. 142:4: "I look to the right and watch, but there is none who takes notice of me; no refuge remains to me, no man cares for me." Jesus' words of prayer strongly suggest The Psalms, particularly Ps. 5 and Ps. 71.

Give ear to my words, O LORD;
    give heed to my groaning.
Hearken to the sound of my cry,
    my King and my God,

for to thee do I pray.
O LORD, in the morning thou dost hear my voice;
in the morning I prepare a sacrifice for thee, and watch.
(Ps. 5:1 ff.)

Mark closes the episode with the arrival of Judas leading a crowd with swords and clubs and accompanied by the chief priests, the scribes, and the elders. It is not an idea alien to Old Testament Scripture that a kiss could be the sign of betrayal. II Samuel 15:1 ff. is the story of Absalom's betrayal of David. He kissed those who were willing to betray David: "Thus Absalom did to all of Israel who came to the king for judgment; so Absalom stole the hearts of the men of Israel." Likewise, Joab stabbed the head of David's army, Amasa, when he grasped him to kiss him (ch. 20:9 f.).

There is true irony in Mark's narrative of the severed ear. One of the disciples, presumably, struck off the ear of the slave of the high priest. With all Mark's references to seeing and hearing, it does not take much imagination to recognize the symbolism. Israel no longer had an ear to hear the message of the Christ. She no longer had an ear with which to hear, and the word would be preached to her no more.

Mark speaks of no contrition on the part of Jesus for the injury to the man. (Cf. Matt. 26:52; Luke 22:51.) Instead, he speaks only of Jesus' anger. The underhanded manner in which the priests had contrived to seize Jesus was what angered him. "Have you come out as against a robber, with swords and clubs to capture me? Day after day I was with you in the temple teaching, and you did not seize me. But let the scriptures be fulfilled." (Mark 14:48 f.) The disciples forsook Jesus and ran, as they had avowed they would not do. Only one followed Jesus, a young man. Him they also attempted to seize, but he ran away naked, leaving them holding his linen cloth. There is a tradition that the young man was Mark himself. It was probably at his house that the disciples ate the Passover meal, and, his description being very similar, the passage may also be intended to convey that it was the same young man at the tomb who greeted the women who came, Mark, the author himself.

The Trial

The stage is set for the fulfillment of the Scriptures, as Mark's Jesus stated, chiefly the prophecies of Isa., ch. 53, concerning the treatment of the Suffering Servant, and Ps. 22. In the three predictions of the final hours placed in the Gospel, Mark had said first that Jesus would be rejected by the chief priests, the scribes, and the elders and put to death (Mark 8:31); next, that he would be delivered into the hands of men and killed (ch. 9:31); and the third prediction stated that he would be delivered to the chief priests and the scribes, who would condemn him to death and deliver him to the Gentiles (ch. 10:33). They in turn would mock him, spit upon him, scourge him, and kill him.

Jesus' remarkable silence throughout the entire proceedings proclaims the fulfillment of the prophecy of Isa. 53:7: "He was oppressed, and he was afflicted, yet he opened not his mouth; like a lamb that is led to the slaughter, and like a sheep that before its shearers is dumb, so he opened not his mouth." His one confession was to the high priests when he affirmed that he was the Christ, Son of the Blessed (Mark 14:62). While Jesus otherwise maintained silence before the high priest, Peter, down in the courtyard, denied any knowledge of Jesus. His terrible denial was brought home to him with the crowing of the cock. Except for the "mourners" in the incident of the raising of Jairus' daughter, Peter's tears are the only tears that are shed in the entire Gospel of Mark.

Mark states that, following a consultation of the whole Jewish council the following morning, Jesus was bound and delivered to Pilate, who asked him if he was King of the Jews. Jesus replied only, "You have said so." It is as if Mark intended to make clear the idea, "You said it, not I." Pilate, perceiving the envy of the priests, which had motivated them to get rid of Jesus, was unable to convince the crowd that Jesus should be released. They had been stirred to a frenzy by the priests, who urged them to ask for the release of Barabbas instead. Barabbas, jailed for insurrection, epitomized the popular longing for a messiah who would bring about political deliverance. Pilate, to appease the angry crowd, released Barabbas and delivered Jesus to be crucified.

The Crucifixion

Mark's crucifixion account is graphically dramatic. After Jesus had been hanging on the cross for three hours, Mark says that there was a darkness over the whole land until the ninth hour. In the ancient world, darkness in the daytime was commonly associated with epochal events. Darkness occurred at the disappearance of Romulus, the death of Casear, etc.

Finally at the ninth hour, Mark says that Jesus uttered a loud cry and breathed his last. "And the curtain of the temple was torn in two, from top to bottom." (Ch. 15:38.) With the symbolic severing of the ear in Gethsemane, Mark has declared that Israel would no longer hear the word, and even that which she had has now been taken away from her, for with the rent veil, God's *shekinah*, the cloud of God's presence, has left the Temple and the Spirit of his presence has gone to dwell in the world.

Jerusalem has been "deserted" by God, and the world has become his dwelling place. The word of God has been delivered from the bondage of old Israel and the sterility of the law. God's presence leaving the Temple is a symbol of its destruction, for without God's presence the Temple would be unclean (profane). All that remained behind him was the law, to which Israel had given a higher place than the word of God brought by his Son.

The sundering of the Temple curtain falls between the death of Christ and the confession of the Roman centurion—that which had been held captive so long in the hands of Israel is now made manifest to the world. The centurion was the first individual to perceive the true nature of the Christ. Recognition of Mark's Jesus as the Son of God came first from a Gentile.

The number of Old Testament references that could be garnered relating to the trial and crucifixion of Jesus is practically endless, but Isa., ch. 53, and Ps. 22 appear to be the chief contributors. The only words Mark attributes to Jesus during the crucifixion are the opening words of Ps. 22: "My God, my God, why hast thou forsaken me?"

Summary and Conclusions

The similarities between Paul's arrest in Jerusalem and that of Jesus have already been pointed out. Paul had been beaten by an enraged crowd, but was rescued by the Romans. Jesus had been the victim of the enraged cries of the crowd, and would have been "rescued" by the Romans had Pilate been able to persuade the crowd to accept his release instead of that of Barabbas. Paul was falsely accused of having taken a Gentile into the Temple, but there were no corroborating witnesses. Jesus' accusers could not even find any testimony against him, and eventually settled for the false charge of "blasphemy" for which they could not obtain witnesses against him who were in agreement, thereby making the charge illegal.

In the final analysis, it was Paul's missionary bias and enterprise that brought about his downfall at Jerusalem. So it was with Mark's Jesus. It was Jesus' fulfillment of the one role to which Israel had been called in the Old Testament covenant, and which she had steadfastly refused, which precipitated the end for him. Jesus was the new Jonah, a Jonah who did not pay mere lip service to the covenant commission, and that only under threat of death, but a Jonah who understood from the beginning the implications of being God's chosen Son, united with God in covenant for service to mankind.

Much of the symbolism of the trial and crucifixion have their foundation in The Book of Jonah. Pilate assumes the role of the mariners on the ship who were forced by the tempestuous sea to toss Jonah overboard. Matthew has gone out of his way to make the point clear when he releases Pilate from blood guilt with the hand-washing episode, much as the mariners pointed out to the Lord that they were innocent of Jonah's blood since it pleased God, not them, to toss Jonah into the raging sea. It was the tempestuous crowd that forced Pilate to toss Jesus to his death. The weeds wrapped around Jonah's head become the crown of thorns placed on Jesus' head (Mark 15:17). Jonah's anguish and sense of separation from God while in the grip of death are no less really portrayed than are Jesus' sufferings and sense of betrayal by God as he hung on the cross, for Jonah, cast into the deep, cried, "I am cast out from thy presence" (Jonah 2:4), and Jesus cried, "My God, my God, why hast thou forsaken me?" (Mark 15:34). After three days in the bowels of death, Jonah was resurrected and kept, albeit reluctantly, his vow to preach the news of God's reconciling love to the Gentiles

(Nineveh). So with Jesus. After three days, just as Jonah was no longer in the belly of the great fish but was vomited out on dry land, so, Mark says, the tomb is empty—it had given up Jesus, and he had gone to preach the good news in Galilee of the Gentiles, where those who would keep the covenant would follow.

Forty days after Jonah's deliverance from the belly of death, he expected to see the destruction of the Gentile community. But the community believed Jonah and turned in repentance to God, who repented of their destruction. Whether or not the Sanhedrin sat and watched for forty days to see whether or not the heretical group of Jesus' followers would dissipate is only an interesting idea, but at the end of forty days, had they been watching, according to the book of The Acts, they would have seen that the community was imbued with the Spirit of God which enabled his word to be preached to the Gentiles, who in turn, repented and believed, and became the Christian church. "And the surviving remnant of the house of Judah shall again take root downward, and bear fruit upward; for out of Jerusalem shall go forth a remnant, and out of Mount Zion a band of survivors. The zeal of the Lord of hosts will accomplish this." (Isa. 37:31 f.)

Mark's Jesus came calling men to decision in such an urgent manner that all who met him found it impossible to be indifferent to his call. Those who were confronted by the Christ found their lives in crisis and were unable to remain neutral concerning his person or his message. Jesus came with authority, giving men a last chance to decide for God's trustworthiness, and any turning away from him was a turning away from God's call to faith. Man must decide, when confronted by the Christ event, whether or not Jesus' witness to the reconciling, caring love of God can be trusted, whether God himself, the final power, can be trusted to hold good intentions for human life.

"The [resurrection] is nothing else but the expression of the right understanding of the Jesus of the days before Easter. . . . Christian faith is not belief in a miracle; it is the confidence that Jesus' witness is a true one. This faith is not made easier or more difficult by the occurrence of a miracle."[43] The resurrection faith is simply a confession that Jesus is the living Word of God and provides the clue to a proper understanding of life.

EPILOGUE

THE GOSPEL OF MARK is one of new life rising out of sinister plotting, betrayal, and death. From the first charge of blasphemy (ch. 2:7), culminating in the plot of the Pharisees and the Herodians to destroy Jesus (ch. 3:6), the Gospel is a crescendo of approaching doom for Jesus, accompanied by the antiphonal overtones of the death of John the Baptist. It was Jesus' threat to the bureaucracy of Judaism which aroused their animosity, and while it is the story of the death of Jesus, it is no less a depiction of the death of orthodox Judaism, as far as Mark is concerned.

The whole of the Gospel is Mark's portrayal of Jesus' attempt to project his vision of the Kingdom to a small group of followers. His own ministry was carried out on the fringe of the Jewish community, and much of it took place in Gentile country. A specific case is made for the acceptance of Gentiles into the Kingdom. Right to the end, however, there was never demonstrated any clear-cut understanding by the disciples of the true import of their call. Mark again and again depicts them as obtuse and without comprehension. In the end they betrayed and deserted Jesus. After his death, they do not even appear in the Gospel, but the last word passed on to them through the women at the tomb, coming from the young man there, was that Jesus had already gone before them into

Galilee of the nations and it was there that they would see him at work. Peter and the others did return home for a while, but felt called back to Jerusalem. It would appear from other sources that they were unable to shake the hold the recent events had on their lives. The book of The Acts describes a breakthrough of understanding, the realization that new self-understanding was possible through the teachings of Jesus Christ. Through him there was indeed new life.

While Peter appears to have done some missionary traveling, the New Testament does not indicate that the understanding of the gospel that is central in Mark ever *fully* came to fruition in any of the original disciples. James, the brother of Jesus, and John did not go out into the world, to the nations, with the good news. They settled in Jerusalem and established there the headquarters of Jewish Christianity, over which James ruled until his death. This group was composed of Jews who also professed Christianity, and while they were jealous of any tampering with their own communities, they made no great attempt to carry the gospel to the Gentiles, and any which they did make was not in the spirit of Mark's Jesus, but was rather a proselytizing of Gentiles into Judaism.

The mission to the Gentiles, clearly the central issue in Mark's Gospel, fell to another Jew-turned-Christian, Paul, who interpreted the gospel in no other way. He believed himself called to carry the good news to the Gentiles and spent his life with that as his foremost goal. There seems little doubt that it was his purpose to carry the good news to the four corners of his world, i.e., to all the Mediterranean countries. While much of his time was spent with Jewish Christian communities, he gradually built up a following of Greek Chirstians, and eventually spent time in Rome with the Christian community there, which was probably a mixed community. There was, apparently, a great deal of antipathy between Paul and James, and

Paul's quarrel with Jerusalem was lifelong. His visits to Jerusalem were rare.

He of all the apostles was the only one who met the resurrected Christ in or near Galilee, for he was on the road to Damascus, which runs through Galilee, right along the shore of the Sea of Galilee. As a minister to the Gentiles, he understood the meaning of becoming a servant after the manner of Jesus' teaching. He could boast, "I have made myself a slave to all" (I Cor. 9:19). He understood the meaning of being released from captivity to the law and of his role as a servant of the covenant. Jesus' teaching was accepted by him: "You know that those who are supposed to rule over the Gentiles lord it over them, and their great men exercise authority over them. But it shall not be so among you; but . . . whoever would be first among you must be slave of all. For the Son of man also came not to be served but to serve, and to give his life as a ransom for many" (Mark 10:42 ff.).

Peter, on the other hand, apparently confined himself to a mission to the Jews. He never completely broke with either Jerusalem or tradition. After James's death, the Jewish Christians found themselves to be a despised minority among the Palestinian Jews, and James was soon forgotten. Eventually, caught in the conflict between Judaism and Roman rule, the Jewish Christians moved their headquarters to Pellas, ca. A.D. 68, and finally faded from the scene, and the only Christian mission that survived was that of Paul to the Gentiles. The power of Judaism in Jerusalem itself was flickering when Mark wrote, and whether or not he foresaw its imminent demise in history, he foretold its spiritual demise in his Gospel. Through years of persecution and martyrdom the Gentile Christians not only survived, but after Constantine, became the religious force that shaped Western culture.

APPENDIX

Mark 16:9–20

Spurious Ending

IT IS NOT DIFFICULT to see why the spurious ending
of Mark (ch. 16:9 ff.) was added by some discerning
spirit. Mark ended his Gospel in the same spiritual tenor
as Isa., ch. 11, i.e., the gathering of a remnant which
would be a sign for the nations. The earth would indeed
"be full of the knowledge of the LORD as the waters cover
the sea" (Isa. 11:9), and in that time:

The wolf shall dwell with the lamb,
   and the leopard shall lie down with the kid,
and the calf and the lion and the fatling together,
   and a little child shall lead them.
The cow and the bear shall feed;
   their young shall lie down together;
   and the lion shall eat straw like the ox.
The suckling child shall play over the hole of the asp,
   and the weaned child shall put his hand on the adder's den.
They shall not hurt or destroy
   in all my holy mountain;
for the earth shall be full of the knowledge of the LORD
   as the waters cover the sea.

                                                  (Isa. 11:6 ff.)

So, along with a borrowed account of the resurrection, someone has concluded Mark's Gospel:

> Go into all the world and preach the gospel to the whole creation. He who believes and is baptized will be saved; but he who does not believe will be condemned. And these signs will accompany those who believe: in my name they will cast out demons; they will speak in new tongues; they will pick up serpents, and if they drink any deadly thing, it will not hurt them; they will lay their hands on the sick, and they will recover.
>
> (Mark 16:15 ff.)

NOTES

1. Robert H. Charles, *Eschatology: The Doctrine of a Future Life in Israel, Judaism and Christianity* (Schocken Books, Inc., 1963), Chapter V.

2. Henri Daniel-Rops, *Jesus and His Times*, tr. by Ruby Millar (E. P. Dutton & Company, Inc., 1954), p. 405; Stanley B. Frost, *Old Testament Apocalyptic* (London: The Epworth Press, Publishers, 1952), pp. 12, 66, and 82.

3. Sigmund Mowinckel, *He That Cometh*, tr. by G. W. Anderson (Abingdon Press, 1956), p. 299.

4. For a penetrating analysis of "St. Luke's Genesis," the interested reader is referred to the article of that name by M. D. Goulder and M. L. Sanderson, which appeared in the *Journal of Theological Studies*, N.S., Vol. VIII, Part I, April, 1957, pp. 12–30.

5. Vincent Taylor, *The Gospel According to St. Mark* (London: Macmillan & Co., Ltd., 1952), n. 1, pp. 177–178; Walter Bauer, *A Greek-English Lexicon of the New Testament and Other Early Christian Literature*, ed. and tr. by William F. Arndt and F. W. Gingrich (Fourth Ed.; The University of Chicago Press, 1952), p. 534; Frank W. Beare, *The Earliest Records of Jesus* (Abingdon Press, 1962), p. 32.

6. Ulrich W. Mauser, *Christ in the Wilderness* (Alec R. Allenson, Inc., 1963), p. 87.

7. Robert H. Lightfoot, *Locality and Doctrine in the Gospels* (Harper & Brothers, 1938), pp. 111 f.

8. Taylor, *op. cit.*, p. 174.

9. For an interesting study of the sequential relationship of the healing narratives not undertaken in this book, see Austin Farrer, *St. Matthew and St. Mark* (London: The Dacre Press, 1954).

10. Cf. Austin Farrer, *A Study in St. Mark* (London: The Dacre Press, 1951), Chapter X.

11. Taylor, *op. cit.*, p. 187; also Beare, *op. cit.*, p. 72.

12. Taylor, *op. cit.*, p. 190.

13. Arnold Toynbee, *A Study of History*, Abridgement of Vols. I–VI by D. C. Somervell (Oxford University Press, Inc., 1946), p. 523.

14. Mowinckel, *op. cit.*, Chapter X.

15. Cf. John Bowman, *The Gospel of Mark* (Leiden: Firma E. J. Brill, 1965), pp. 45 ff.

16. *Encyclopaedia Britannica* (Encyclopaedia Britannica, Inc., 1961), Vol. 20, p. 5.

17. C. Milo Connick, *Jesus, The Man, The Mission, and The Message* (Prentice-Hall, Inc., 1963), p. 151.

18. Bowman, *op. cit.*, pp. 46 ff.

19. *Encyclopaedia Britannica*, Vol. 7, pp. 227 f.

20. *Ibid.*

21. W. D. Davies, *Paul and Rabbinic Judaism* (London: S.P.C.K., 1955), p. 37; Joseph Klausner, *From Jesus to Paul* (London: George Allen & Unwin, Ltd., 1944), p. 299.

22. Taylor, *op. cit.*, p. 202.

23. *Ibid.*, p. 210.

24. *Ibid.*, p. 238; also Bowman, *op. cit.*, p. 129.

25. Taylor, *op. cit.*, pp. 238 f.

26. Bauer, *op. cit.*, p. 368.

27. Bowman, *op. cit.*, p. 146.

28. Bauer, *op. cit.*, p. 496.

29. Taylor, *op. cit.*, p. 296.

30. *Ibid.*, p. 297.

31. Erwin R. Goodenough, *Jewish Symbols in the Greco-Roman Period* (Pantheon Books, Inc., 1956), Vol. V, pp. 31 f.

32. *Ibid.,* p. 91.

33. *Ibid.,* pp. 81 ff.

34. Taylor, *op. cit.,* p. 357.

35. Bowman, *op. cit.,* p. 179.

36. Leander E. Keck, "The Introduction to Mark's Gospel," *New Testament Studies* (London: Cambridge University Press, July, 1966), Vol. 12, No. 4, p. 363.

37. For a salient discussion of this portion of the Gospel, see Farrer, *A Study in St. Mark,* pp. 113 ff.

38. Bowman, *op. cit.,* pp. 213 f.

39. The number of times Mark uses the figure "three" in his book is remarkable. The Gentile crowd was with Jesus three days at the second feeding; there were three withdrawals by Jesus; there were three predictions by Jesus of his death, all in a similar context; three times Jesus returned to the disciples in Gethsemane after prayer, and three times they were sleeping; there is emphasis throughout on three particular disciples; Peter denied being a follower of Jesus three times; the prophecy of resurrection is couched in terms of three days after the crucifixion.

40. There has been little attempt in this book to discuss the symbolic meanings of the names of either people or places, although these are all surely significant, as is the geographical route Jesus took to Jerusalem, which can in many respects be demonstrated to be similar to the route of Joshua upon crossing the Jordan. For a more detailed discussion of the symbolism of names and places, see Farrer, *A Study in St. Mark, passim.*

41. R. H. Lightfoot, *The Gospel Message of St. Mark* (Oxford: Clarendon Press, 1952), pp. 60 ff.; also, Frederick C. Grant, "The Gospel According to St. Mark," *The Interpreter's Bible,* ed. by George Arthur Buttrick, *et al.* (Abingdon-Cokesbury Press, 1951), Vol. VII, p. 830.

42. Bauer, *op. cit.,* p. 381.

43. Van Austin Harvey, *The Historian and the Believer* (The Macmillan Company, 1966), p. 274.